Arm in Arm with Adolescent Girls

HORIZONS *IN* RELIGIOUS EDUCATION is a book series sponsored by the Religious Education Association: An Association of Professors, Practitioners and Researchers in Religious Education. It was established to promote new scholarship and exploration in the academic field of Religious Education. The series will include both seasoned educators and newer scholars and practitioners just establishing their academic writing careers.

Books in this series reflect religious and cultural diversity, educational practice, living faith, and the common good of all people. They are chosen on the basis of their contributions to the vitality of religious education around the globe. Writers in this series hold deep commitments to their own faith traditions, yet their work sets forth claims that might also serve other religious communities, strengthen academic insight, and connect the pedagogies of religious education to the best scholarship of numerous cognate fields.

The posture of the Religious Education Association has always been ecumenical and multi-religious, attuned to global contexts, and committed to affecting public life. These values are grounded in the very institutions, congregations, and communities that transmit religious faith. The association draws upon the interdisciplinary richness of religious education connecting theological, spiritual, religious, social science and cultural research and wisdom. Horizons of Religious Education aims to heighten understanding and appreciation of the depth of scholarship resident within the discipline of religious education, as well as the ways it impacts our common life in a fragile world. Without a doubt, we are inspired by the wonder of teaching and the awe that must be taught.

Jack L. Seymour (co-chair), Garrett-Evangelical Theological Seminary

Dean G. Blevins (co-chair), Nazarene Theological Seminary

Elizabeth Caldwell (co-chair), McCormick Theological Seminary

Dori Grinenko Baker, The Fund for Theological Education & Sweet Briar College

Sondra H. Matthaei, Saint Paul School of Theology

Siebren Miedema, Vrije Universiteit Amsterdam

Hosffman Ospino, Boston College

Mai-Anh Le Tran, Eden Theological Seminary

Anne Streaty Wimberly, Interdenominational Theological Seminary

Arm in Arm with Adolescent Girls

Educating into the New Creation

EMILY A. PECK-MCCLAIN

PICKWICK *Publications* • Eugene, Oregon

ARM IN ARM WITH ADOLESCENT GIRLS
Educating into the New Creation

Horizons in Religious Education

Pickwick Publications
An Imprint of Wipf and Stock Publishers
199 W. 8th Ave., Suite 3
Eugene, OR 97401

www.wipfandstock.com

PAPERBACK ISBN: 978-1-5326-3478-9
HARDCOVER ISBN: 978-1-5326-3480-2
EBOOK ISBN: 978-1-5326-3479-6

Cataloguing-in-Publication data:

Names: Peck–McClain, Emily A.

Title: Arm in arm with adolescent girls : educating into the new creation / Emily A. Peck–McClain.

Description: Eugene, OR: Pickwick Publications, 2018 | Series: Horizons in Religious Education | Includes bibliographical references.

Identifiers: ISBN 978-1-5326-3478-9 (paperback) | ISBN 978-1-5326-3480-2 (hardcover) | ISBN 978-1-5326-3479-6 (ebook)

Subjects: LCSH: Teenage girls—Education—Religious aspects. | Teenage girls—Education

Classification: LCC LC1481 P3 2018 (print) | LCC LC1481 (ebook)

Manufactured in the U.S.A.   06/27/18

Dedicated to the girls of the New York Annual Conference,
who dared to trust me with their stories

and

dedicated to my own two girls,
I will always fight for your freedom in Christ

CONTENTS

SERIES FOREWORD

Religious Education Association

HORIZONS in RELIGIOUS EDUCATION defines a book series sponsored by the Religious Education Association: An Association of Professors, Practitioners and Researchers in Religious Education. The REA founded this series to promote new scholarship and exploration in the academic field of Religious Education. The series includes both seasoned educators alongside newer scholars and practitioners just establishing their academic writing careers.

Books in this series reflect religious and cultural diversity, educational practice, living faith, and the common good of all people. They are chosen on the basis of their contributions to the vitality of religious education around the globe. Writers in this series hold deep commitments to their own faith traditions, yet their work sets forth claims that might also serve other religious communities, strengthen academic insight, and connect the pedagogies of religious education to the best scholarship of numerous cognate fields.

The posture of the Religious Education Association has always been ecumenical and multi-religious, attuned to global contexts, and committed to affecting public life. The REA establishes these values in the very institutions, congregations, and communities that transmit religious faith. The association draws upon the interdisciplinary richness of religious education connecting theological, spiritual, religious, social science, and cultural research and wisdom. *HORIZONS in RELIGIOUS EDUCATION* aims to heighten understanding and appreciation of the depth of scholarship resident within the discipline of religious education, as well as the ways it impacts our common life on a fragile world. Without a doubt, we are inspired by the wonder of teaching and the awe that must be taught.

—Dean Blevins, former president of REA and Professor of Practical Theology and Christian Discipleship at Nazarene Theological Seminary in Kansas City, Missouri, U.S.A. Co-chair, Horizons Editorial Board

PREFACE

We are pleased to announce this fourth book in the Religious Education Association, HORIZONS series. Dr. Emily Peck–McClain of Wesley
Theological Seminary in Washington, DC focuses on faithful ministries to
adolescent girls. As we know, the world is a difficult place for adolescents
today—school violence, family concerns, and bullying as well as the risky
state of the globe. Through ethnographic research, Dr. Peck–McClain invites
us into the lives of several adolescent young women. We hear their assess-
ment about the state of the world and how it affects their lives. Furthermore,
she offers directions from her faith community of how to respond to these
young women and invite them into the depth of faith resources.

Every faith tradition struggles with how to influence the lives of
adolescents. They wonder how the faith is communicated so that it makes
sense and invites young people to grow in faith. We hear a lot in the
popular press about the "nones" and the "dones" people who have lost
connection to a religious tradition or those who have intentionally left
a religious community behind. The research however clarifies that these
persons have not necessarily left spiritual struggles behind—they seek to
answer questions of meaning and vocation as well as to engage spiritually
with the others and the world.

This reality profoundly affects young persons. Can they trust the communities of faith that seek to nurture them? Does religious faith make sense
considering their studies? How do faith commitments shape their identity
development and claiming of vocation—we know many are committed to
enhancing our communities and environments? And even if these questions are answered in the affirmative, we are still faced with the issue of
whether religious communities are adequately addressing the brokenness

in the world and whether they are faithfully passing on a meaningful and profound faith tradition.

Today many groups are exploring the dynamics of adolescent faith and religious formation. For example, several theological seminaries in the U.S. sponsor programs for adolescents seeking to offer faith, meaning and vocation. With the publication by Donna Frietas of *The Happiness Effect: How Social Media is Driving a Generation to Appear Perfect at Any Cost*, the National Study of Youth and Religion enters into its fourth wave of research on the religious lives of youth in the U.S.[1] The Yale Center for Faith and Culture is sponsoring a major project on Adolescent Faith and Flourishing.[2] And the Lilly Endowment has just funded several studies of young adult experiences and ministries.[3] The dialogue is rich and provocative.

Into this context, Christian educator and practical theologian, Emily Peck–McClain probes the riches of her Christian tradition to see how Christian formation can provide both support and resources for young people. Beginning with ethnographic data of adolescent women, she then turns to the profound theological work of a founding disciple of Christian faith, St. Paul asking how his reflections on faith and decision-making, offered to the first century world, can be refocused as a guide for young people. Her work is an amazing project of Christian religious education and practical theology analyzing the experiences of some contemporary adolescents, drawing on the rich scholarship in Christian religious education and youth ministry, and probing a founding theological source. She offers direction for the ways we think about youth ministry, how congregations can shape Christian formation, and how we invite young people to use tools of faith to understand and engage their world. Finally, she closes with a brilliant letter (epistle) to adolescent girls offering hope and direction.

---

1. See Donna Frietas, *The Happiness Effect: How Social Media is Driving a Generation to Appear Perfect at Any Cost* (New York: Oxford University Press, 2017). See the the home page of the National Study on Youth and Religion, http://youthandreligion. nd.edu/. Also see the archive of research studies that has been collected, http://www. thearda.com/Archive/NSYR.asp.

2. See "Adolescent Faith & Flourishing," http://faith.yale.edu/adolescent-faith-flour ishing/adolescent-faith-flourishing.

3. See the December 9, 2016 press release from the Lilly Endowment, "New Initiative to Help Congregations Find New Ways to Engage and Support Young Adults." http://www.lillyendowment.org/pdf/YoungAdults12-09-16.pdf. In fact, Dr. Peck–McClain is involved with such a grant at Wesley Theological Seminary. See https://www. wesleyseminary.edu/wp-content/uploads/2017/01/D821621.Letter_Proof-2-2.pdf.

We commend this book to you. The Religious Education Association in founding the *HORIZONS in Religious Education* series sought to offer books grounded in a religious tradition to offer concrete ways to affect our public world. We believe that religious education is at its best when it is grounded in a formative religious tradition, it reads the signs of the times, and it seeks to offer ways to enhance public living. This book certainly does all of that. Christian educator and theologian, Dr. Peck–McClain provides religious leaders and scholars with a model for how persons of faith draw on and reshape their religious resources for religious education, faith formation, and public living.

—Jack L. Seymour, Professor Emeritus of Religious Education at Garrett-Evangelical Theological Seminary, Evanston, Illinois, U.S.A. Co-chair, Horizons

—Elizabeth Caldwell, Adjunct Faculty, Vanderbilt University Divinity School, Nashville, TN, U.S.A. Co-chair, Horizons Editorial Board

EDITORIAL BOARD

Class of 2017

—Dean G. Blevins, co-editor, Nazarene Theological Seminary, Nazarene Theological Seminary, Kansas City, MO, U.S.A.

—Sondra H. Matthaei, Saint Paul School of Theology, Leawood, KS, U.S.A.

—Siebren Miedema, Vrije Universiteit, Amsterdam, The Netherlands

Class of 2018

—Elizabeth Caldwell, co-editor, Vanderbilt Divinity School, Nashville, TN., U.S.A.

—Dori Grinenko Baker, The Forum for Theological Exploration, Atlanta, GA, U.S.A.

—Anne Streaty Wimberly, Interdenominational Theological Seminary, Atlanta, GA, U.S.A.

Class of 2019

—Jack L. Seymour, co-editor, Garrett-Evangelical Theological Seminary, Evanston, IL, U.S.A.

—Hosffman Ospino, Boston College, Chestnut Hill, MA, U.S.A.

—Mai-Anh Le Tran, Garrett-Evangelical Theological Seminary, Evanston, IL, U.S.A.

ACKNOWLEDGMENTS

My love of Paul began with taking a course called "The Apostle Paul" in Spring term of my junior year in college. I am deeply grateful for the content of that course and for Alexandra Brown, its instructor, who has continued to support me in my studies of Paul and in my vocation since. Her love of Paul and the clarity of her reading of were both contagious.

I am extremely grateful for my dissertation committee for reading through chapters, bearing with me as dates shifted, and spending their time, energy, and wisdom on my education. I am humbled by their taking my work seriously. Thank you to Susan Eastman, Evelyn Parker, and Mary McClintock Fulkerson. At the head of that committee was Fred P. Edie, who has been a tireless dissertation supervisor, academic advisor, mentor, and friend in my years at Duke and since. "Thanks" does not seem a sufficient word.

My thanks also to my mom, Dawn Peck, my first and last editor and my best cheerleader. I also want to thank Joyce Mercer and Dori Baker, both of whom gave me the gift of their time, insights, and guidance at different stages of my work. I truly benefit from their work and their willingness to consider me a colleague. For the nuts and bolts of this project, which I could not have figured out on my own, I thank TWB, Jonathan LeMaster-Smith, Joel Harding, Chris Gonzalez, and Elizabeth Bendler Bannon. The headaches you saved me cannot be counted.

The majority of this book, in its prior dissertation form, was written during my year as an American Association of University Women (AAUW) Dissertation Fellow. I am grateful for their support, but am mainly grateful for their tireless efforts of empowering women and girls. I am honored they see me as part of their important work.

This book was brought to life by the careful and patient work of editors Jack Seymour and Elizabeth Caldwell. I can only describe Seymour's involvement in this process as midwifery. Thank you to both of you for your insights, careful attention, and constant challenging encouragement.

Andy, my patient and supportive partner, I thank you. You have always believed in me and my work, sometimes for the both of us.

INTRODUCTION

You chose the kind of friends you wanted because you hope you could be like them and not like you. To improve your image, you made yourself more stupid and less kind. As the months passed, the trade-off for belonging started to feel too great. The shutting down of some vital part of yourself, just so you could be included on a shopping trip into town, not have to sit on your own at lunch or have someone to walk home with. Now among friends, you were often lonelier than you had been before. The hierarchy of girls was so much more brutal than that of boys. The boys battled for supremacy out on the pitch and, after, they showered away the harm. The girls played dirtier. For girls, it was never just a game.

—ALLISON PEARSON, *I THINK I LOVE YOU*[1]

Youth ministry is big business. It is lots of fun. It is heart-wrenching. Youth ministry is a faithful way to respond to the needs of teenagers and their families. Youth ministry is glorified babysitting. Youth ministry is pointless. Youth ministry is a constant struggle against the pressures of other extra-curriculars. It is an important safe space for teenagers. It is self-absorbed. It only works in big churches. It requires too many adults to be consistent with safe sanctuary policies. Youth ministry doesn't matter to the rest of the church. Youth ministry offers youth a space to grow in their faith. Youth ministry is a place to make sure your kids don't lose their faith.

I have been in youth ministry long enough to hear all of these and more, and to say some of them myself. There are *a lot* of different ideas

---

1. Pearson, *I Think I Love You*, 136.

about what youth ministry does, should do, and can do. The truth is that in whatever conversations I have about youth ministry and in whatever books, articles, and blogs I read about youth ministry, one thing is clear: youth ministers and youth ministries need something else to help them lead the vibrant ministries youth and their families need. This book aims to fill some part of that need. Here I offer a way to be in ministry with adolescent girls, their families, and their churches that equips folks with a theological and biblical lens intended to be deep and complex enough to see and act upon all the deep and complex needs adolescents and the people who love them have.

Adolescence, no less than any other life stage, involves moments of joy and moments of sorrow, times when faith is sure and times when faith is shaky. Adolescence also sometimes gets dismissed. We live with the legacy of the "storm and stress" idea—of course adolescents are unhappy, adults seem to say (or actually do say), that's what being an adolescent is![2] Well-meaning adults often try to offer advice that amounts to minimalizing adolescents' difficulties by keeping everything "in perspective": your life isn't over because some boy broke up with you, there are other fish in the sea; you don't need to be popular to have a good time in high school; it's not the end of the world; of course you're in a bad mood, it's just hormones. At the same time, however, adolescents are always told just how important this time in their lives is. They are told to work hard in school, not have sex, stay away from drugs, alcohol, gangs, violence, R-rated movies, the "wrong crowd," wearing revealing clothing, and myriad other dangers that have the possibility to ruin their lives if they are not vigilant. Adolescents are picking up on these mixed messages from the adults in their lives, their parents, caregivers, pastors, youth workers, and others. So which is it? Does adolescence matter or not? Do adolescents matter or not?

I recall one evening, when I was working as a youth minister, when a teenager came to my house late one night because she was dealing with a tough situation at home and needed to talk. She was in tears and then stopped, wiped her eyes, and said, "I'm sorry. I know it doesn't even matter. There are people out there who are dying of hunger." I think of another youth who often asked me to drive her home after youth group because otherwise she couldn't come. She never invited me inside, and one day she

2. This is a common view of what adolescence involves since G. Stanley Hall published the concept in 1904. Although it has been widely disproven as a determinative feature of adolescence, the expectation of it still looms large for parents.

finally told me why. Her family didn't have any furniture because of the effects of her father's gambling addiction. She was embarrassed and scared and completely powerless to change the situation.

These are just two of the many situations I have walked through with adolescent girls throughout my years in youth ministry. Just two of the situations with which I have been challenged to find the resources I need to put these struggles into conversation with the faith of adolescent girls. Where is God when a girl does not know if her problems, which are very real to her, actually matter? Where is God when a girl's father has a gambling addiction? Of course the "good Christian answer" is that God is with both of those girls. And that's true. And that's also not always enough. These girls need a way to understand why this is happening. Why is home life difficult? Why are people dying of hunger? Why does my father gamble? Of course these are the big questions of theodicy that are eventually and finally unanswerable for us.

Theodicy is the question of how bad things can happen in a world created by a good God. Theodicy is the question of why bad things happen to good people. Theodicy is Job asking God why he suffered so very much. These are the big questions. These are also the kinds of questions Christians have been struggling with and bringing to God for centuries. They also seem to be the questions that many churches, youth ministries included, are particularly ill-equipped to offer guidance for how to confront.

There are good reasons for this. It is scary for adults and teenagers alike to delve into unanswerable questions. Sometimes what happens in life is at odds from what we've learned about God growing up in churches. Sometimes what happens in life feels "inappropriate," or perhaps, "unacceptable" for church. Adults who are tasked with being leaders in youth ministries may not have any answers themselves for these big questions. Youth deal with life in bold color and do not yet have the filter that adults have.

Be a caring adult in youth ministry long enough and you will hear the very deep and real concerns of young people, some of which might make you uncomfortable. Youth might ask questions adults have not asked themselves. Adults might believe that they must have concrete answers for youth to all the questions they ask. If the questions are unanswerable, that can be a really difficult position for an adult who has that belief.

There are other reasons, too, why youth ministries can be ill-equipped to welcome the hardest questions that youth have and help offer a viable theological lens for these teenagers. In looking at the majority of youth ministry curriculum, Christian education for teenagers usually consists of teaching basic tenants of one's faith tradition and moralistic life lessons designed to keep young people safe during the potentially life-threatening period of adolescence. These are wonderful things to teach adolescents, and there is much more that needs to be a part of their Christian formation in order to help their faith speak to their life and their life speak to their faith.

Additionally, for years youth ministry has been based on understanding the development of adolescents. Understanding adolescent cognitive, social, and psychological development is extremely helpful to know how to present different ideas to youth and in realizing why they may be acting in certain ways. Like Christian education based on teaching a faith tradition and instilling morals, knowing these developmental theories and bringing their insights to bear on faith formation of adolescents in the local church is extremely helpful and leads to better ministry young people. Developmental psychology, however, is not the same as Christian education.

Many in the world of youth ministry, perhaps the most well-known being Kenda Creasy Dean and Andrew Root, have been researching and designing ways to bring theology into youth ministry ethos and curricula. This new emphasis is a wonderful addition to the study and practice of youth ministry. This approach emphasizes that what youth ministries teach about how, for example, the choices teenagers make, relationships they have, and ways they think about. However, there is still more we can do to welcome the real lives of our teenagers into the church and make certain that the formation we are effecting helps them live their lives in a spiritually, emotionally, and theologically healthier way. The truth is that Christianity has what teenagers need in order to make sense of their lives and face all the joys and challenges that are a part of it. However, the church has not always been effective in offering this kind of robust Christianity to them. Of course this begs the question of whether or not the church actually proclaims Christianity, at least in all its powerful and complex layers, which exist for the powerful and complex nature of our lives.

From the time I spent in conversation with the 24 girls I was privileged to interview for this project it is clear to me that this is often the case.[3] The church is often missing the opportunity to help girls live a robust faith and empower them through that faith. Sometimes this lack is caused by the real and pressing concerns parents and other caregivers have for the safety

---

3. Please see the appendix for more information about these girls and the interview process.

of their children. They want their children to stay safe and make good decisions. They want them to lead moral lives. The problem is that these teenagers are aware of moral ambiguity and are not being invited to bring that awareness into conversations in their churches. Sometimes churches themselves are not equipped to teach adolescent girls a reading of Paul that is anything other than moralistic or even sexist.

The world of youth ministry has been aware for years of the need for teenagers to have meaningful relationships with adults and not be ghettoized in "youth spaces" that enable them to so easily age out of church rather than stay in it. We have learned that teenagers need adults to look up to, to see what they can become as adult people of faith. The truth is that youth need adults for more than those reasons. Youth need adults because being a teenager is hard. They need open relationships with people who will care for them rather than judge them. They need to be loved. And when it comes to the very real difficulties teenagers face, they need allies in the fight against those that threaten their humanity. It's that serious. The church is called to be active in the world, one way to do that is through ministry with our young people who are on the front lines of consumerist culture and inundated in their formative years (though, of course all years are formative) by a society that tells them their value is in their looks, their money, their fitting a gender expression norm, and other aspects that have nothing to do with their God-given worth as a created being of the One Creator.

And then there's the way the church has failed to offer an alternative, or has compounded the problem. Adolescent girls carry particular burdens in this area. Christianity has not been empowering to young women. In fact, it has been the opposite. Girls have long been saddled with the expectations of purity and virginity in a way different from boys. Girls who are finding third and fourth wave feminism empowering for their lives outside of church find it absent in the church. In a way, every conversation I had with these young women had their embodied lives at the center. They were aware of and connected to their bodies, even when their bodies were something to be feared or a source of stress. Their faith is embodied, their theology is lived in the skin they inhabit. The church's silence about their embodied existence was often as loud as the spoken messages they received from adults in their churches.

I was listening to NPR in early 2011 and heard an interview with author Allison Pearson, who had just published her novel about teenage life in England. I really wasn't interested in this book until she read an excerpt from it, the excerpt I placed at the top of this chapter. I ordered it that day from Amazon.com. She put into words what middle school felt like to me.

When I was in middle school, I was active in a youth group led by passionate and caring adults and college-age volunteers. I went on retreats and work missions. I was an acolyte. I continued to be active in church through middle school and high school. I was baptized at the beginning of high school, but already by then some part of myself was going deep into hiding. This was the kind part. The vulnerable part. The passionate part. I desperately wanted my classmates to like me for who I was, but that wasn't happening. I did not like my budding breasts, and tried to hide them by wearing oversized shirts and slouching my shoulders. I stopped combing my hair because I thought I was unattractive and didn't want to fail and trying to be attractive, so I went for the opposite. It would give me an excuse if boys didn't want to go out with me. It was clear that the expectation was for girls and boys to be dating and to be attracting and impressing each other. I was sure I would fail at that if I tried, and kind of hated that I was even supposed to try.

I remember in seventh grade a boy made fun of me for not shaving my legs, so I started shaving my legs and hated that I did. I remember getting an outfit that I thought was unbelievably cool. And being made fun of relentlessly for it. So I tried to do the opposite of me. I saw the girls with whom I wanted to be friends. They were confident and expressed the anger that I was feeling. They didn't seem to care what others thought of them. Like the quotation above expressed—I wanted to be like them and not like me. Inside I was scared and angry. I liked learning. I liked being a little naïve. I still wanted to be nice to others and have others be nice to me. But let's be honest, the Golden Rule doesn't seem to apply in middle school.

Eventually, I did start to become friends with these girls who were so unlike me but so like I knew I needed to be to survive. This friendship came at a high cost, it cost me myself. I remember one day walking around a neighborhood with these four other girls. One of them spit on me. From what I could tell at the time, it was "just because." Probably something they had seen happen or heard about and wanted to try. I stayed friends with them. Maybe that's what proved my allegiance to them, because from that point on I was "in." But I wasn't happy. My family was dealing with a lot of turmoil. My group of friends wasn't actually that nice to me, and I didn't know who I was anymore. But Sundays at youth group, I still smiled. I had trusted counselors who cared about me and listened to my pain without flinching. When I needed a safe haven, the adults and college counselors in the youth group provided it. I had people who told me the truth. Looking back, this was one of the only ways the spark of who I was deep inside remained lit.

I don't think I let that vital part of myself come back to life until I was in college. Why this happened might be partially explained through developmental psychology; adolescence can be a challenging time. How part of myself went into hiding and nearly died is also a theological problem, one that, no matter how active I was in youth group and church, was not solved. Although my youth group loved me and provided a safe place for me, I did not learn how to think theologically about my life. I did not know what was going on developmentally, socially, or spiritually. I did not know how to value and trust and love myself. I did not know how to nurture myself. I only wanted to hide myself, change myself, and survive. Youth group was not connected to the real struggles I was having. I did learn that I should give some of the money away I earned waitressing, should not have sex before marriage, and should generally treat people nicely. For all the good it provided, I still did not have the tools to understand what was going on in my life, or how to respond to it in healthy way.

Middle school was brutal. High school was not much better, though at least I could see life after high school on the horizon. I was not the only girl who struggled through these years. I needed help. I was not learning how to handle it or how to maybe even make it less brutal for myself and others. These realities are still true for many girls, even though it has been a long time since I darkened the hallways of middle or high school.

Then I met the apostle Paul—not in a Bible study, a sermon, or a youth group lesson, but in a college classroom. Reading his letters opened my eyes to a way of processing my teenage years and current struggles. I found the theological lens I had so desperately needed in middle and high school. Here was someone who understood that life was brutal, gave a reason why, and told us in no uncertain terms that not only will it get better, we can also actively fight against this brutality. Here was someone who wrote with passion I found missing even in the most passionate-for-Jesus youth ministry expressions of faith. Here was someone who lived in the real world. The professor of that class was a woman who would become my academic advisor and my senior thesis advisor. She pushed me and encouraged me, and has continued to do so. She was the one who opened Paul up to me in a drastically new way. The whole Bible seemed different after reading Paul now. I had a new way to talk about what was so hard as a teenager and what was so hard at the present. I had a new way to talk about what was so good as a teenager and what was so good at the present.

I also began working as a youth director while I was in college and have continued working with youth ministries in some capacity ever since. I constantly see the need for Paul's perspective in the lives of adolescents. In every youth group I have worked with, the struggles adolescents face have been woven into my heart. Their stories, even decades after my own adolescence, connect to my own stories. Life is not going to be without struggles; not for anyone, including adolescents. Life is going to be harder on some than others, especially given the ways this society continues to be an oppressive one for women and girls, immigrants, people of color, LGBTQ people, and many others. After years in youth ministry, having girls come to my office hating their bodies, feeling like their worth was wrapped up in their relationships (or lack thereof) with boys, seeking to be accepted for who they are, and staring down eating disorders, cutting, addiction, rape, and a multitude of other adversities, I grew increasingly frustrated that my books and curricula did not have anything to help them. I did my best. I loved them. I welcomed their stories and held them as sacred. I prayed with and for them. I cried with and for them. But I felt ill equipped, even after a seminary education, years of experience, and a passion for God. This is from where the inspiration for this project arises.

This project is, at its core, about listening. I spent several months listening to adolescent girls. Yes, these conversations could be called interviews, but it is more accurate to say that they were sacred spaces where girls were brave enough to share their stories, hopes, dreams, questions, faith, lack of faith, and vulnerabilities with me. I was prepared to have some of their stories remind me of my own adolescence. I was prepared to have some of their stories surprise me because my adolescence was unlike theirs. There was no Instagram when I was a teenager. Or smart phones. And I grew up in the mountains of Virginia, not in and around the city of New York. I was prepared to be impressed with their thoughtfulness and somewhat envious of their assuredness.

I was not prepared for the depth with which they would open up to me, a stranger to most of them. I was not prepared for the deep place within me that they would touch. I should have been prepared for that, after so many years working in youth ministry and knowing that these conversations were happening in the context of an academic project. But there was nothing

8

academic about their stories. Everything was profoundly theological, personal, and holy. I heard secrets and pain and joy and hope.

In writing this book I hope to meet adolescent girls in this place of real questions and real formation. As Allison Pearson wrote in her book, there is a brutality to being a teenage girl, not only in their social hierarchies, but in the structures of our society at large and the church. What girls experience as teenagers is written into their identity going forward. This includes how they feel about themselves, what parts they try to hide or cover up, how small they try to become because of the pressure to do so, how they understand and value (or not) their bodies, and in what way their bodies are or are not encouraged to be a part of the faith they are developing. Here I offer a theological lens that is particularly well-fitting for adolescent girls; one that comes right from our foundational source for such things, the Bible. This lens, provided by Paul of all people, and the method I suggest for helping girls to use this lens can help adolescent girls understand their realities in a theological way and respond in life-giving ways to them.

In some ways, this is an exegetical project. I do a close reading of the lives of these girls as they share them with me alongside a close reading of Romans 6–8. The exchange between the girls and Paul's worldview demands tools for the empowerment of adolescent girls. This exegetical conversation requires action. Therefore, in other ways this is a practical project that calls for action on the part of adolescent girls, adult women, and the church as a whole. This is a call for a change in how we educate and form all the members of our churches and how they, in turn, are called to act differently in the world outside of the church as well as inside of it. In the face of societal and familial pressures, including the ways the systems of racism, sexism, classism, and heterosexism that threaten their humanity, sense of self, and often their safety, we as the church are called to do something once we have heard fully and deeply the stories that illustrate these experiences. Paul's way of seeing the world is a powerful and unused resource for these girls who are seeking to understand their lives. What comes from making use of this resource with adolescent girls is a practice of story sharing and interpretation, liberative ministry, and community formation, not only for girls, but also for the church in which they are members.

The girls with whom I spoke have showed me not only their stories and the ways the church can help them, and often isn't, they have also showed me the profound gifts they have for the church and the world. They have a critical eye toward the world around them. They are often aware of hypocrisies that exist in the church, their school, social expectations, and their families. They are frustrated by double standards that they see operating around expectations and assumptions about boys and about girls. They have a passion for life, an excitement and an energy, that is almost palpable when speaking to them about their lives and their faith, about what matters most to them. Like most children and young people, they are not quite as cynical and resigned to the status quo as adults can be. They are honest. They want to tell their stories and to be heard; they know the value of speaking. They have vibrant spiritualties. They are not idealistic about the world around them, and yet maintain hope in the future. They are fun and funny. They see the world in bright colors, rarely in black in white. They are thoughtful and take the asking of questions about themselves seriously. These characteristics are strengths for being able see in the way that Paul sees, maybe even more clearly than the adults who would seek to lead them.

chapter 1

THIS BODY OF MINE

I spent the summer of 2013 driving and taking public transportation all around the New York Annual Conference of the United Methodist Church. This geographic area spans New York City, Long Island, Western Connecticut, and New York's Hudson Valley (on both side of the river) almost as far north as Albany. My time was divided into two-hour interviews with twenty-four adolescent girls ages 12–19. Each conversation I had was a gift. I learned so much about the individuals, their communities, and their experiences. I welcomed their anger, confusion, hope, and passion. I found myself in awe of their wisdom and honesty, and about how much they care about their churches, families, friends, and the world. Sometimes I spent those conversations thinking about how I could hear my own experiences as a teenager echo in their words. Sometimes I felt like I could not have had a more different adolescent experience. Each time I felt I was on holy ground in those church basements, youth rooms, coffee shops, cafés, and apartments.

The racial makeup of the group is fairly diverse. I asked the girls to share with me how they describe their race; here are their self-reported answers: Eleven girls are white; four girls are African American; two girls are Asian American; three girls are Latina American (one of whom mentioned she is the first in her family born in the United States); three girls are Caribbean American (one of whom mentioned that she immigrated to this country when very young); one girl is half Latina and half Spanish. Two of the three Caribbean American girls also self-identify as Black.

Of all these young women, I have chosen to spend significant time focusing on Sam, Sadie, Tay, Brooke, Raven, and Genevieve. Although any of the girls would have fit as focus points for this project, these six girls were diverse in their theological commitments and life experiences, thus forming an interesting sample on whom to focus. About half of the interviews were conducted one-on-one, the other half were conducted in groups. This sample group of six accurately reflects that split: three were interviewed in a group, three were one-on-one. Although these girls are not meant to be representative of all adolescent girls or even all adolescent girls in the New York Annual Conference of the United Methodist Church, they do illustrate clearly some of the common challenges adolescent girls are facing now. Their stories show opportunities for how the ideas of Pauline theology can enrich the lives of girls of different backgrounds and social and theological locations. Sam is Asian American, Brooke is Latina American and Spanish American, Raven is Caribbean American, Genevieve, Tay, and Sadie are white. These girls are from varying socio-economic backgrounds, ranging from lower middle to upper middle class.

Sam and Sadie both attend the same church. They have been attending their church for as long as they can remember and are friends outside of their involvement in church activities, although they attend different high schools. They both live near their church. Sam is 17 years old and a junior in high school. Sadie is 15 years old and a freshman in high school. I knew both of these girls prior to the interview.

When asked about her ethnicity, Sam describes herself as Asian and as "a banana." When asked to share more about what that means to her, she says, "yellow on the outside, white on the inside. I don't know, I don't really see myself as Asian, though. I don't see myself as anything else . . . I am Asian. I do like my skin color." Sam was adopted from her birth country by two white American parents. She lives in a predominantly white neighborhood. She attends a school with a diversity of races and cultures and where her group of friends is not white. Sam lives with her mother, father, and younger sister, who was also adopted from an Asian country. When asked about her sexuality, Sam responded that she is gay, something she has known about herself "ever since I was little." She came out to her parents in eighth grade. She describes this process as going "fine." Her mother works for a computer company in another state, but works mostly from home. Her father is a stay-at-home dad.

Sadie lives with her father, mother, and younger brother. When asked about her ethnicity, Sadie responded, "I'm white. I know . . . it doesn't sound good to say I wish I wasn't white, 'cause that shows a lack of understanding. Because it's a lot easier to be white. And that's why I wish I wasn't white."

Like Sam, most people in Sadie's neighborhood are white, but most people in her high school are not. When asked about her sexuality, she responded, "Oof, I wish I knew ... It bothered me so much that I couldn't, like I couldn't tell if I was gay or if I was straight, and then so I was like I'm bisexual, because that's both. And then I decided that, like, I'm neither ... But then my brother, like, he's always saying like, 'Sadie's gay,' but that bugs me because I'm not gay. I don't literally like boys, but I don't feel gay." Her parents are both professionals, working for nonprofits.

Brooke describes herself as 50% Spanish and 50% Latina. Her parents are deceased and she lives with her aunt and uncle, both of whom are retired. She moved in with them once her mother passed away when she was 11. Her mother passed away from complications from surgery for a condition from which she herself also suffers. A year ago, she underwent the same surgery that resulted in her mother's death. She is 16 years old. She also has an older half-brother, with whom she has not lived since their father died when she was 3. She describes her sexuality as "straight." She and her mother tried attending churches when she was younger but they never found one that they liked. She began attending her local United Methodist church when she moved in with her aunt and uncle because it was the church that they attended.

Genevieve is a member of the same church as Brooke. The two of them were part of a group interview, along with three other girls from their church. She went through Confirmation Class with Brooke and both of them joined the church after that class ended. Genevieve is 17 years old and in her junior year in high school. She lives with her father, mother, and two brothers. Her mother has a part time job, which Genevieve could not specify. Her father works for a manufacturing company. She describes her ethnicity as "white" and her sexuality as "straight." She was brought up in her local United Methodist Church and says that she always attended and went to Sunday school. She has lived in her town for her whole life.

Raven is 18 years old. Our interview took place during summer vacation after she had just graduated from high school and was preparing to attend a state university in the fall. Her interview was also a group interview, along with three other girls from her church. She moved to the United States from the Caribbean country in which she was born 13 years ago with her mother. Her father and his family remain in that country. She has strong ties to that country, its culture, and its food. She has been attending her local United Methodist Church since she came to the United States. Her mother works as a financial representative for a hospital. It is clear that she and her mother struggle some financially. She states that her mother "believed in the whole 'American dream' you could find a better life living here . . . Which is completely a lie." She describes her sexuality as "straight."

Tay is 17 years old and also just completed her senior year in high school. She plans to attend community college for two years and then transfer to a design school where she wants to major in photography. Her parents both work at different stores. Her father is a salesman and her mother works as a receptionist with some responsibilities for book-keeping. She was looking for a job at the time of our meeting so that she could buy a car in order to get to her classes at college in the fall while living at home with her parents. Tay has had a difficult relationship with church. Her church has gone through several different pastors in her time involved there. One of her previous pastors, who was there during Tay's confirmation, was known to be ineffective in ministry. Tay described how this situation caused her father to stop being involved in the church until their current pastor was appointed about a year ago. Tay herself also has some difficulties with the attitudes of some of the members of her local church whom she calls judgmental. She has been active in a denomina-tional Christian formation program that involves retreat weekends and small groups. This is where she finds the most support for herself and her faith. When talking about her ethnicity, she refers to the many Euro-pean countries from which her family ancestry originates. She describes her sexuality as "bisexual," something that she has only recently come to terms with and has not shared with her parents.

Of the many topics we covered in these interviews, a few stand out as the ones around which the girls were most energized. As I present the stories of Sam, Sadie, Brooke, Genevieve, Raven, and Tay, along with several other girls, I do so around these topics. Whether asked explicitly about them or asked seemingly unrelated questions, girls' experiences seemed often to stimulate mention of these topics. The qualities of resil-ience, critical thinking, engagement, and willingness to tell truth all come through in conversations surrounding these especially important topics. These separate but connected topics contribute to the picture of what life is like for these adolescent girls. Their own words about these topics most important to them demonstrate their emerging sense of identity, their critical thinking skills, their faith formation, and their general perspec-tives on the world.

These parts of our conversations show what these girls are struggling with and how they think through the problems with which they are faced. Also clear in these conversations is that girls are ready to share their wisdom and experiences openly when asked and when their answers are taken seriously. They have so much to offer the church, they are as much as part of the church as any other mem. Practical theologian Joyce Mercer in her book *Girl Talk/God Talk* concluded that girls do not separate out faith from other subjects when they share their stories.[1] I found the same to be true in my conversations with these girls. Their faith is woven seamlessly into their conversations about school, home, friends, and current events. I can see, however, that for some adults, this integrated faith might seem surprising. Adults often excuse faith from some of the messiness of life. Adolescent girls welcome their faith to unexpected places. So although these topics are all topics of faith for them, I have divided the topics into two groups for the purposes of discussion. The first set of topics, covered in this chapter, are the topics having to do with being an embodied human being. More specifically, these topics are "Clothing the Body," "Racism," and "Sexism." Because they are Christian, the challenge of understanding and appreciating themselves as embodied includes how to think about their bodies in the context of their faith, even as some of them critique the way faith is lived out in their churches in regards to bodies.

CLOTHING THE BODY

The girls I interviewed often voiced complex emotions about their bodies, which are changing and beautiful and complicated. Many girls talked about their bodies with grief or disappointment. Many talked about their bodies with defensiveness or confusion. Some talked about their bodies with appreciation or even awe. Nearly all of them told about experiences with comments and looks they have received in response to their bodies and clothing. These responses come from peers and from adults, sometimes in church settings and sometimes in school or social settings. Girls' perspectives on and experiences through their bodies were connected to their understanding of their faith.

I found these girls often concerned with their appearances. They talked a lot, whether prompted by a question or not, about clothes, body image, and how their appearance is received by others. They were well aware and

1. Mercer, *Girltalk/Godtalk*, 125.

critical of what lies beneath the surface of their appearances and others' responses to their appearances. Through these conversations, I heard sharp critiques of consumerism, the fashion industry, pressure to have a certain body type, generational differences, sexism, racism, and other assumptions made about them based on appearance. I also heard their desire to be attractive. Girls are not thinking surface level when it comes to their appearances. Neither did these conversations stem from self-absorption, as is often assumed from topics like this.[2]

Adolescent girls experience their lives as embodied. They do not see their bodies as separate from their emerging identities, but rather integral to it. Social historian Joan Brumberg writes that for contemporary adolescent girls, the body is the site of expression of the self, "[t]he body is a consuming project because it proves an important means of self-definition, a way to visibly announce who you are to the world."[3] Womanist theologian M. Shawn Copeland explains the value of the body to one's experience as a Christian, stating that "the body is the site and mediation of divine revelation."[4] The body, then, is an essential way to express oneself, to be in the world, and to experience and understand the Holy. This is no less true for adolescent girls than it is for adult men and women. For the girls I interviewed, their bodies are an important way they experience their lives and a lens through which they seek to understand their faith and their faith communities.

They learn a lot about their bodies from the media, of course, but also from their churches. Connecting the body and soul together in a positive way is unusual in Western Christianity, which tends to negate the body or to view it as inherently problematic or even dangerous to a person's spiritual life. This view of particularly the female body as problematic or dangerous is shared by American culture as well.

I met with Sadie in the youth room at her church. She appeared confident and energetic. She was eating some granola and yogurt and was immediately chatty. When I asked Sadie what makes her faith journey more

2. "All too often, the passage of adolescent girls is viewed as inevitably problematic. All too often, media and societal attention have focused on how girls look or their presumed self-absorption with appearances . . . As we go beyond the appearance of adolescent girls into their competencies, their relationships and their communities, we see opportunities to enhance their voyage and ways to ease their passage," Johnson and Roberts, "Passage on the Wild River," 4.

3. Brumberg, *Body Project*, 97.

4. Copeland, *Enfleshing Freedom*, 2.

difficult, her answer was quite succinct, "I would say myself," she responded. I asked her to say more and she indicated that she is weak, emotionally and physically, and that she doesn't like herself sometimes. She sees places she has grown in her life so far, noting that, for example, watching movies used to very troubling for her but that she is able to not get quite so upset by what she views as she used to. She also recognizes that she can see emotions as a possible strength of hers. But growing beyond disliking herself in terms of her appearance is something with which she still struggles. She said, "I get frustrated with the way I look. And I can't do anything about it, I mean I can try. And I tell myself that I can do stuff about the way I look, but I can't really." I asked her what she would change and she said, "I think I'm too fat." When I asked her more about where she has received messages about being fat, she mentioned people in school who had told her she didn't dress right or gave her tips about where to buy jeans. She mentioned a girl she spent her summers around who would always ask her how much she weighs. She also mentioned that until late in middle school she did not feel that she had friends who really liked her, she says she felt annoying to them. In her mind, being annoying to others was connected to her weight.

I also met with Sam in the youth room at her church. She walked in with her bike, which she had ridden to the church. To me she appeared calm and curious about what the interview was going to be like. During this interview, I was the one who brought up clothing in order to see what Sam's thoughts were on the messages girls receive about clothing. I asked her about what kind of clothes she wears and she indicated that no matter what she was doing, she basically wore the same kind of comfortable clothes. Then I asked her about what she sees other girls wearing, her response was that society has made her judgmental when she sees what other girls wear. She clarified that the first impression she gets of some other girls based on their clothing is that they are "sluts." She said that she makes this judgment based on their clothing, that they wear so little clothing, they may as well be wearing just underwear to school. I asked her why she thinks girls wear this kind of outfit and Sam responded, "Um, I mean people see it as they want attention, but then, . . . I don't know how to put this, um, you also have the people who say, you know, girls should be able to wear what they want, you know, and not have guys just holler at them . . . But for girls at my school, I don't know. It sort of does feel like they want the attention. Or they want to show off something."

This tension that Sam alludes to is common for the girls I interviewed. Girls want the freedom to wear what they want without judgment or undesired attention, but at the same time, they are aware that sometimes girls do choose their clothing in order to get some kind of attention. Is it an exercise in freedom to wear whatever one wants? Should there be limitations? If so, what are they and who sets them?

One of the group interviews I did included five Black girls—African American and Carribean American. We met in their youth minister's house around some pizza she had ordered for them before disappearing so we could talk without her present. When I asked them what they wish was different about their church, the subject of dress came up immediately. Two of the girls, Beverly and Monica, were sisters. They sat next to each other and encouraged each other while they shared. Beverly, who is sixteen, said that the church was judgmental, specifically around what girls were expected to wear, which she says is covered up and wearing "ankle skirts and stuff." Raven, however, noted that girls with different bodies have different expectations placed on them. The continuing conversation took place between Raven, Beverly, and Monica, who is nineteen.

Raven began by pointing out that body type matters in the conversations around appropriate and inappropriate clothing at her church. She gave the example that if she and another girl wore the same dress but the other girl was skinnier, she would get called out for wearing something inappropriate, "But they don't take the time to look at it that way. They just see, 'Oh look at her boobs and her butt all out! I can't even concentrate!'" She also said that the expectations for clothing for girls is not realistic. People at her church have told her that her dresses need to go below her knees. "I'm 18 years old, where am I going with below-my-knees dress? Like, they don't even sell that for 18 year olds! It's so annoying! But then, like, I bet you if a skinny girl put on the same dress, but it went above her knees, she's not bulging-out bodies so it's not gonna, like, show. You know?" Beverly pointed out that people from her church have talked to her mother about her and her sisters' outfits, saying that they should dress more appropriately and cover up more. She then said in frustration, "But I mean, and my grandma buys all our dresses! So, come on, like, I don't think it's that bad!" I asked these girls what they thought the people in their church were objecting to when it comes to how they dress. This was the response:

Beverly: They want us to dress like them.

Raven: My personal issue is that I can't, the reason why I have a hard time agreeing with it sometimes 'cause I don't know if this whole dressing rule is man-made or like God said. In other words . . . why is a skirt here so wrong? Is that because adults don't like it, or is it because it's inappropriate to God himself? Like, how do we know, like, I feel like you're just telling me to do cause you don't like it. But I don't, I think, I don't know, I think in my head it's like, I'm here in church so God is happy with me just being in church. I didn't come here completely naked. I'm wearing clothes.

Monica: I agree with Raven, though, because like, I see some rules like that as man-made because, like, I feel like especially there's a lot of stress, like, the church will put on females and the way they dress and stuff like that. Um, and I think that's not even so much for our well-being like, you know, I'm not saying to come to church with like your butt and boobs hanging all out, but, like, if you, like, I feel like even if we do show a like little bit of shoulder or something like that, back then, that was like a big deal. Because of how it was perceived like it was scandalous. And why was it scandalous? Because it was considered like a seduction or whatever. So I see that more as a, like, being a man-made thought, like, we're taught to hide our bodies because, I don't want to say cause men can't control themselves, but because, it's considered tempting to like, you know, people. And I feel like that's not, I kinda want to say, I don't want to say, I mean, it's not fair. But, at the same time I'm not saying, you know, go out naked. But I'm just saying, like, don't put restrictions on what we wear because some people can't control themselves. You know?

This interchange is full of important aspects of the girls' lives and how they process what they experience. They are concerned about the ways girls and women are treated differently from men and boys. They experience this difference through the expectations placed on what they wear to church and how different female bodies wearing the same thing are received differently by people in their churches. They do not want "restrictions" put on them around clothing because they feel they are capable of making their own decisions around such matters and being appropriate in their choices. Moreover, they see these restrictions as "man-made" rules that are put in place in order to somehow protect men who can't control themselves. The conversation involves their faith. If it were a God-made rule, presumably they would feel differently about it, but they see it as a man-made rule to protect men from the temptation that their bodies (and how they are clothed) provide.

Raven points out that girls with different body types have different expectations placed on them about how they will clothe that body. She seems frustrated that her own curves make her seem sexually provocative in a dress that would not be considered sexy for a skinny girl. The critical eye with which these girls are evaluating their experience about clothing and church shows how adolescent girls are able to pick up on hypocrisy and will point it out. They are asking important critical questions such as, do these rules come from God or from men?[5] Why might those rules be there? Why are rules different for some bodies than others? Why are rules put in place against women because of the actions of men?

Raven also points out how what girls choose to wear is often dictated by the marketplace, and not by free choice. However, she is uncritical of the marketplace for making this decision for her because she seems to not want to wear anything longer than what she sees sold in stores. I wondered if she would be more critical of the marketplace's offerings if it did not offer something she wanted. This was the experience of Tay. She pointed to the fashion industry as a part of her experience in her body. She is critical of consumer culture, and clothing is the way she experiences it. The marketplace has presented a challenge for her own acceptance and understanding of her body, as well as for her friends. Tay was quite interested in the subject of bodies and clothing; it came up in our conversation without my prompting. Having been directed to the topic by her English teacher, she had just finished her senior term paper on it.

> Tay: . . . [T]he fact that, I've grown up being overweight constantly I've realized that there are very, very judgmental people when it comes to like the fashion industry and, um, being in high school when you're being overweight you're always being judged . . . And, the fact that you're a woman doesn't help, and, I'm always in between sizes, because of the way that my body is. And, there is nowhere that has clothes that fits me perfectly. So, I'm always getting either a size too small or a size too big. So, that's always been an issue for me, and my friends are always saying, "Oh, you're just not looking hard enough." I'm like, "No. There is no pair of pants that fits me perfectly.

5. Generally I avoid using gendered language and would instead write "humans" here. However, based on the conversation, I think it more accurately conveys the girls' meaning to use the term they themselves chose—"men."

Me: So . . . the fashion industry tells you to wear and they don't even offer you something to wear?

Tay: Yeah. And the fact that they don't even have clothes to fit us . . . Like, you're creating more of a kind of a risk for teenage girls going more towards eating disorders than losing the way [that is] healthier because they wanna lose it faster. So they can be in perfect weight for bathing suit season or summer. Just so they can fit in the bikini. Like it's putting more pressure on girls than it needs to, that's why there is a higher rate of girls killing themselves and girls cutting themselves and girls having eating disorders, because there's more pressure on females to look hot instead of to look natural . . . It's putting more pressure on girls to wear make-up and to look hot instead of looking like you're comfortable in your own body.

Because most of my friends have told me they are not comfortable in their own bodies no matter what size they are. [One friend is], like, a size zero, [another friend is] a size six or something like that . . . And we always get into arguments about that, and all of my friends hate the way that they look. And the fact that I have to hear my friends say that and them being absolutely beautiful is making me feel horrible because, what does that make me? And, the fact that society is still bringing that upon teenage girls, it's making it harder for us to continue that message of being perfect the way you are, you're beautiful no matter what.

Like Raven, Monica, and Beverly, Tay has a critical eye toward the way that bodies and clothes are viewed. Her focus in this part of our conversation was around the fashion industry and sizism, along with the way that her friends talk about themselves. Also like Raven, however, she is missing a piece of her critical awareness. She seems to have bought into the societal definition of beauty as thinness, at least for white women, when she points out that her friends who are size 0 or size 6 are "absolutely beautiful." I do not doubt that her friends are beautiful, but a greater critical awareness on Tay's part would express that their beauty (and hers) is not about a clothing size.

Elsewhere in our conversation Tay spoke about how her church responds to her clothing. She mentioned that, except in the summers and holidays when people are visiting from elsewhere, she is the only teenager in her church. In her area of the Conference, there is a large presence of a denominational ongoing youth gathering, which she has found more helpful for fellowship and formation because she has the opportunity to be with other youth. This gathering includes weekend experiences of spiritual growth and formation followed by opportunities for small group interaction after that experience, as well as continued participation in other weekend-long events as an alumna. She describes the event as involving people who care about her and can help in ways her church does not because they are "very judgmental because it's all older people." When I asked her how this comes out in church, she pointed to several different situations, including disapproval in the congregation of her pastor being engaged to a non-Christian woman and people in her congregation saying that same-sex relationships are "disgusting," when her view on the issue is quite different. She also pointed to how her clothes have been received. She has been criticized for not wearing dressy enough outfits to church. She remembers one time in particular where she came to church dressed in a short-sleeved shirt and jeans because there was a church clean-up day scheduled for after worship and she did not want to have to change clothes. A woman in her church rolled her eyes when she saw Tay, and then Tay heard her tell her husband, "She's not dressed appropriately, I would send her home if she were my child." One of the ways Tay deals with this kind of thing is by sitting away from other people in the church. She controls the laptop and projector for worship, which requires her to sit at the very front of the church. She said that she likes sitting up front "because I can't see people like whispering and judging and all that."

Although clothing and bodies are on the minds of many adolescent girls, this is far from the only thing about which they are concerned. There has long been an assumption that adolescent girls are preoccupied with their appearance. From the evidence offered by the interviews I conducted, their concern about bodies is not an unhealthy self-absorption but an exercise in developing their own critical lens and a struggle to understand the different messages they both receive and wish to send. There are certainly pieces of the conversations that show that girls struggle with how to like the way they look, but this is not the main point of their talking about bodies and clothes. Rather, these points of tension around how a girl looks or dresses are actually about sexism, pressures from churches, society, and traditions, and the effects of the marketing of the fashion industry on how girls view themselves. The negative messages girls receive about their bodies and clothing become incorporated into their developing sense of self. These messages are often also received from their religious communities. When this happens, girls also incorporate these messages into their faith.

Adolescent girls are sensitive to hypocrisies and unafraid to point them out. However, practical theologian Katherine Turpin notes that as their identities are forming, adolescents are less likely to be able to see the hypocrisies in their own personal commitments.[6] This may be part of what is going on when Raven is not critical of the fact that there are no dresses for her to buy that would go below her knee or when Tay voices a comment how her thinner friends and their beauty, showing that she has absorbed some of those messages she wants to fight against.

RACE AND RACISM

Like all other people in this country, adolescent girls interact with perceptions, prejudices, and questions about race constantly. During the interviews, I asked girls to describe their ethnicity. I chose this question carefully, leaving room for the girls to interpret it according to their experience and understanding. Many girls asked for clarification of the question, to which I would reply that in other interviews some girls gave the answer of their race and some people offered their cultural or ethnic heritage. Some girls simply answered the question and we moved on to the next question; but for some girls, this was an opening to a larger conversation, as was the case with Sadie. Once she admitted that sometimes she wishes she was not white, she shared with me her awareness of and experience of white privilege. She said, "I feel like sometimes when I'm buying stuff, I like, I get certain, like, respect or reception that like my friends who aren't white don't get." She shared her observation of Black culture and Hispanic culture at her high school and realized that she doesn't really have a culture. Then she corrected herself, "well I guess I sort of do. I don't know, and it was like, it was sort of weird for me because I'd always been around people who [thought] race wasn't even an issue, not that it wasn't an issue, but it just wasn't really talked about because we all assumed . . . we weren't racist or whatever. And then I was like, wait a second, we probably are."

Sadie is aware of a difference in her experience going from middle school, where most of the students were similar to her in terms of "culture," to high school where that was no longer the case. Now that she is a high school where the majority of students are not white, she feels singled out. The experience has also made her aware of white privilege and how racism was a part of her life even when she did not think it was.

6. Turpin, *Branded*, 112.

With Sam, the question of race came up not in answer to my direct question about the topic, but in answer to a different question. When I asked her to describe the place that she lives, she answered, "It's white." Like Sadie, she attends a high school outside of her neighborhood, and one that does not have a majority of white students. She continued to talk about race, her neighborhood, and her own identity as an Asian girl adopted by white parents. She told me that because her parents are white and she lives in a white neighborhood, most people, especially her Asian friends, see her as white. This is part of why she defines herself as a banana, "yellow on the outside, white on the inside." When thinking about her own identity, she ended up by saying, "I don't know, I don't really see myself as Asian, though. I don't see myself as anything else." She is struggling with how to identify herself in conversation with her family's race and the perspective of her friends at school.

She confidently stated, "I am Asian. I do like my skin color." Then I asked her how she responds when she hears her friends saying negative things about white people, which she told me happens fairly often. Sam responded, "Surprisingly I don't feel anything. I'm indifferent to what they say."

Sam has a dual identity as an Asian person with white parents. She alternately describes herself as "not Asian", "Asian," and "a banana." Like Sadie, she experiences comments from her peers about what being white means. Adolescence is a time of identity development. For girls, identity exploration and understanding is a contextual pursuit. A general question of identity does not recognize the reality that adolescents "must negotiate their multiple selves."[7] Sam's challenge to describe her identity is not a simple task. She is someone when she is with her family and someone when she is with her Asian friends. Her description of being "a banana" may be one way she has found to vocalize the multiple selves that make up her identity. Ethnicity is an important factor in identity formation, one that is more complicated for someone like Sam whose ethnicity is different than her parents'. As Sam continues to explore who she is in the different contexts that make up her life, hopefully she will develop a coherent and consistent sense of self, an identity that responds to her experiences in those differing contexts.

Two of the group interviews I held with Black girls ended with my being asked the same question by them: "Do you experience racism?" This was a question I only received from Black girls in my interviews. I wondered

7. Johnson and Roberts, "Passage on the Wild River," 11.

if it was the case that they had little experience talking openly about race with a white person. In response to one of the groups asking that question, I responded that as a white person, when I experience racism it is as a beneficiary of privilege because of my skin color. I gave the example of having an easy time getting a cab when a person of color standing near me would have a harder time. Monica agreed, saying that it often took her a long time to catch a cab in neighborhoods that were majority white. Beverly then asked the group if they think white people on the subway are suspicious of them because they are African American. She points out that people give her "a look," and wonders if it is because of her skin color. Raven pointed out that she thought it was more of an education issue than a race issue, that if white people grow up around people of color, then they will act differently toward people of color than if they grow up around only white people. Monica then related an incident that happened while on the subway:

> [W]hen I took a train for the first time by myself . . . only, like, 2 stops and like, I sat next to this guy and he called me the "n-word." And I was like, I was so taken back, like I didn't know. I think I told Mommy, I don't, it just didn't occur to me how like crazy it was. I just I was so confused because, like, I had never heard, cause I don't use the word. I don't, I don't hear people, well, at the time I didn't really hear people saying it cause, like, I [had gone to] a really like a close-knit Catholic school going into public school, so that in itself was just like a . . . shock. And then for something like that to happen. And the people just stared at me for like 2 stops. And I was just like, "Did he expect me to, did they expect me to, like, say something? Should I have said something? Or what?"

Although Monica relates this incident on the subway as being the "only time" something "like that" has happened to her, she earlier mentioned finding it difficult to catch a cab in a white neighborhood. Unlike Beverly who wonders if white people are suspicious of her on the subway, Monica thinks her experience is different because except for this incident of overt racism, she "doesn't really think about it." Like Monica, Raven says she does not think like Beverly does, but she does relate an experience in high school that shows she is aware of white people's assumptions about her because of her race. In her story, people in her class assumed she was not intelligent because of her skin color. She related that her classmates treated her like she was the "dumbest of the class" and would laugh when she answered a question from the teacher. She said it was actually funny because she would always get the question right and then the others would feel awkward. She also stated that although this happened, she thanks her school for the experiences, both the racist ones like this example from class, but also other ones when she found relationships with white students that showed her another perspective. She said, "My school opened me up to racism at its own, but also opened me up to like seeing maybe seeing the part of whites that maybe Black people don't hear about. That, hey, not all whites hate Blacks." She learned about white people who made fun of her and assumed her ignorance as well as white people who do not "hate Blacks." Issues of race affected all the girls whom I interviewed. Race and racism affect how girls come to view themselves and the world around them. Race is also a part of their faith.

The church that Beverly, Monica, and Raven attend is primarily a Black church. They state that the leadership of their church often talks to them about how the Black community needs to come together to fight the racism with which they are faced. Their awareness of racial issues in the news is keen, partially because these topics are discussed within their faith community. When I asked Raven what makes her angry, her answer was, "injustice." I asked her for a specific example of how she experiences injustice, and her response included recounting a current event of racialized violence. What followed was a conversation between her and Monica that brought up racism by name.

Raven began by talking about a recent killing of a young unarmed black man, which upset her as if she were part of his family. She couldn't believe that someone would get away with killing an unarmed Black man now. She remembered times in school when she had learned about racism in an historical and literary capacity. She said, "seeing it still done today is kinda just, like, it makes you not really have faith in what the generation [is doing] . . . [O]ur generation specifically now, there are some that are so determined . . . make change. And then you have the complete opposite, too." Monica and Raven then went on to discuss several cases of violence against Black people both close to them and farther away as instances where they can see racism clearly. Raven then brought up racism in the educational system:

> Raven: It's things like that . . . Or stuff like in the . . . when they'll put more educated teachers in maybe the more whiter areas of living but then go somewhere like the projects and you catch these broken down old schools where not the top-notch education. And then they'll be like, "African Americans have the lowest SAT rate." Well, duh. Who taught us? Like, where were the other teachers when you want to send us these teachers that barely graduated

THIS BODY OF MINE

college properly. It's just like, all that type of stuff. It's almost like sometimes they set it up to fail. Like in situations like that. I don't know, like, I don't like to see it cause it's just like, they wonder why they can't progress and it's just like it's clear in front of your face.

This conversation shows that these girls experience racism in overt, covert, and systemic ways. Beverly doesn't know if the looks she gets on the subway are because of her race or not. Monica knows that she was called the "n-word" on the train because of her race. Raven is aware of assumptions about her intelligence level because of her race. All of them are seeing racism in their lives, whether on the news or on the train. Raven and Monica area aware of violence against their community, particularly against young Black men. And Raven is aware of how systemic racism affects the quality of education in Black schools. Their church is a place where racism is openly discussed and the members are encouraged to fight it together, thus explicitly connecting this reality to lived faith. Even for those girls who do not have churches addressing race and racism, their attitudes and experiences around race and racism are a part of their identity, which includes their faith identity.

SEXISM

Although the Black girls from that group interview report that issues of racism and current events that stem from racism are talked about in their church, they also report that sexism is not discussed. According to Monica, "It's a taboo subject. But they definitely talk about how as a race, like, you need to you know fight back and do for us." Sexism may be off limits as a topic of discussion in their church, and in other churches as well, it is something that these girls experience regularly in their lives both inside and outside of the church.

Sam brought sexism up, by name, at the very beginning of her interview. She said that she grew up hating the country in which she was born, and from which she was adopted because of "their sexism towards girls." When I asked her to share more about this she said that people there want to have boys because they think boys are stronger and more capable of physical labor than are girls. She pointed out that this makes her extremely angry because she views herself and strong and someone who can work as hard as a guy. I asked Sam if she knew that she was given up for adoption because of her sex, and she said she suspected this was so. Sam then went on to describe how she experiences sexism in her life here, making clear that sexism is not something she sees as only a problem in the country of her birth. She shared with me that her dad is a stay-at-home dad, which is opposite of the stereotypical family. Her friends have told her that her mom should be the one cooking their meals, not her dad.

In one of the group interviews, I asked the girls what makes a girl a good Christian and what makes a boy a good Christian. The five girls all agreed that there was no difference. Britt Nicole compared training to be a good Christian to training to be good in sports. She said that women and men who want to be really good athletes have to train differently because their bodies are different, and likewise there are "different trainings that women and men have to take in their faith journeys because we are differ- ent but going toward the same goal of 'I want to be the best Christian that I can be.'" So although she thinks the goal is the same, she thinks the way to reach that goal is different for women and men.

After her statement, I asked the group what they thought sexism was. Genevieve's answer, like Britt Nicole's about the differences for each sex in becoming a good Christian, recognizes that there is a difference between girls and boys:

> A lot of guys will say, "Make me a sandwich" and that's sexism, like, against, like, women; or saying women can't do things men can do or men can't do things women can do or men belong in the workplace and women are "taking over." Although, like, the news is all like, "Women are now the main people in college." And the main thing, like . . . Anybody who says that women can or can't do something or that men can or can't do something that the opposite gender can or can't do, that is sort of separating the genders and then saying that they're like . . . 'cause to some extent like Britt Nicole said, there is difference you know, like, in gym obviously guys are gonna play harder than most girls and guys are probably going to end up being, like, rougher than most girls. But saying that a girl can't do that and can't play sports at that level or, you know, something like that. Like, completely general- izing, that really affects us.

When asked about the effects of this kind of generalizing, Britt Nicole brought up that she feels like she is treated differently at home than her brothers are because she is a girl. Brooke brought up her medical disabili- ties as something that, when combined with her sex, make it difficult for her to be treated in a way she feels is equal to others. She gave an example of when she's trying to move a chair at church and people in her youth group tell her not to do something like that because she's a girl and has a physical disability. Brooke expressed frustration at others thinking she can't do something when she knows that she can.

Genevieve then connected sexism to racism, remarking that there are differences between skin color just as there are differences between the sexes. She said that "You do have to at some point acknowledge that our skin colors are different. We don't have to be segregated, we don't have to make a difference out of that but we do have to acknowledge that . . . " She is struggling to find a way to acknowledge difference without attaching a value to that difference. She is also struggling with expected gender performance and how it plays out for her. In a conversation with her brothers, she heard some confusion from them about how girls both do and don't want the door held open for them. She said, "[I]t is sort of tough sometimes to think, for me at least, to figure out where the line is when I need to be able to say 'I'm not going to do that because I'm a girl,' because that's not fair, but like, I do want a guy to be nice and hold the door open for me and I don't want to have to say that's because I'm a girl. I want it to be because it's nice, so it's like, sort of a weird line." There was a lot of agreement in the group with Genevieve's statement about the "weird line" that they are walking of wanting to be treated equally and also wanting "chivalry" (the word Genevieve used to describe the kind of behavior like boys opening doors for girls).

In this group, there was an awareness of the complexities of talking about equality and sameness. These girls wanted to acknowledge the difference between the sexes, but did not want there to be judgment attached to those differences. Britt Nicole summed up their collective sentiments on the subject nicely, "it's annoying when it's an oppressive sexism. You know, like, yes we are different . . . But, you don't need to limit the things that I do because of that. And you don't need to look down on me because of it." What this group did not express was a critical awareness of where their desire for "chivalry" might have come from. Certainly the media and marketing industries have had an impact on what girls expect from boys, like doors being held open for them. They also did not see the potential for problems with statements like because of the different between men and women the "trainings" they need in life need to be different. Given her statement that races don't need to be segregated, but they are different, what would Genevieve have said if I asked her if she thought that different skin color means the need for different "trainings" in life and faith also?

Sadie shared several experiences she has gone through that have affected the way she views boys and has brought attitudes boys have toward her as a girl into sharp focus. She has had awareness of the way her safety might be in jeopardy as a young woman for some time. When she was in sixth grade, she started to walk to school alone, with her mother walking behind her. Her mother would then give her feedback about her walk and, "tell me what not to do and what to do, and I wasn't supposed to walk too close to the buildings, people could push me over." If something like that were to happen, her mother warned it would be a defining moment in her life, she said to Sadie, "I just want you to be careful because it'll be a before your life and an after . . . You'll remember that moment." She related one experience on the subway where her fear about what might happen to her turned into what might be termed a conversion experience. She shared this experience as she was talking about how she feels bad for making judgments about people.

> Sadie: Mostly the thing that I mostly make judgments on is based on gender, like if you're a guy and I'm, like, I am terrified. I, I don't even know why, but I'm like really scared of being raped, like that scares me. Well, I mean I guess I have a good reason, I don't know. I think my mom, like, instilled it in me . . . [O]nce I was on the train and I was in the subway and . . . it always stops, like, in between [one street] and [another street]. And, so, anyway, like I was sitting there and I looked up from my book and I realized, like, it was only me and this guy in there, and I was like, "Oh my God, oh my God, oh my God," and that, like, scared me so much, and I was, like, I feel like that's when I decided that God existed. Because, I, I knew, I *knew* this guy wasn't going to do anything to me . . . it was a psychological fear. And he was on the other end of the car, too. But I was just like, "please God, please help me, please," 'cause I was, I don't know why I was so scared, but like, and, so then, I just felt like this thing like settled down on me, and it was like all the seats were full. I know that sounds kind of stupid.

> Me: No, it doesn't.

> Sadie: I don't know, I thought like all the seats were full and that somebody was just smiling at me from all those seats and somebody was like, I don't know. But I felt like a presence, and I was like, "OK, I'm alright, I'm just being ridiculous." And then I got off the train and I went to school.

Sadie also participates in a before school program at her high school for gifted students. She is the only girl in the program, and the school as a whole is also 70% male. She describes how they "fake flirt" with her and how she felt like she couldn't be friends with any of the guys in the program because they might think she likes them. She also felt for the first time that she had to "stick up for myself as being a girl" and prove them wrong for thinking she is not as smart as they are. She also gets teased in a way similar to what Sam and Genevieve report, boys telling her she belongs in the kitchen or that she shouldn't stress out because it might negatively affect her future children.

In the field of psychology, much has been written about the experience of adolescent girls as opposed to adolescent boys in terms of their development during these critical years. This time in girls' lives has been called a time of "heightened psychological risk"[8] when gender stereotypes begin to exert their force. Girls still have to fight against sexism, as these interviews show. Some of their struggle is exacerbated by the expectations the girls hear from people in their faith communities, especially around issues of their bodies and how they are clothed. The girls I interviewed are not from evangelical communities who have been taught about female submission as a biblical instruction, but certainly some of that theology is behind what the girls are experiencing. In fact, Britt Nicole referenced Proverbs 31, which talks about the qualities of a good wife, in our conversation. This outline of a good wife is certainly in line with the traditional female role of running an efficient household and supporting one's husbands. Some of the struggle these girls have with sexism comes from assumptions of traditional female roles in this society. Several girls pointed to specific comments they have heard from their peers about the female's place being in the kitchen.

TEMPTATION

In one of my group interviews, one including five girls, how they thought about temptation, and how boys and girls experience temptation differently, the conversation quickly turned to the clothing that girls wear. They recounted a retreat event they had attended that separated the boys and girls. The girls guessed at what the boys had heard. One girl guessed, "I'm pretty sure it was porn, sex, and stuff." Brooke stated, "They just told us, like, not to bother them. Like, 'don't be tempting' . . . Make sure you don't

8. de las Fuentas and Vasquez, "Immigrant Adolescent Girls of Color," 142.

do this or, like, but I'm pretty sure they were talking to [the boys] like, 'Don't rape them.' I'm pretty sure." Britt Nicole, stated that when it comes to premarital sex, girls are taking advantage of boys, who suffer more temptation than girls do. She thinks that while girls experience peer pressure from other girls like boys do, girls do not also experience temptation from boys. She said, "You know, there are some girls who act like fools and who, you know, don't wear the most modest clothing and, um, make themselves very available and that is another source of temptation. So I think guys tempt each other and girls tempt them and they sort of have it coming at them from all directions."

Genevieve concurred. From her experience on a work mission trip and her conversation with some of the boys in her youth group, she determined that part of her goal as a Christian teenager is to not tempt boys who are trying to be good Christians by her choice of clothing. Genevieve noticed that some girls were wearing tank tops which they had cut the arm holes in so that their sports bras were visible. She expressed some shock that girls would wear clothing like this, but it was something she hadn't really thought too much about until one summer on a work mission trip with her youth group when she got into a conversation about temptation with the boys in her youth group, including her brothers. She reported that the boys were talking about how girls make it difficult for them to be "good Christians." That's when she realized that, "Even just like seeing the bra is just like enough to be like, 'that's temptation!' So I have been very aware of the fact that it is tough for guys who want to be good because I figure the kind of guy that I want to end up with is going to be like my brothers or like these other boys and they say they don't like it when the girls tempt them."

If the body is the "ultimate expression of the self"[9] and the body is a source of temptation to boys, as these girls have been taught and seem to uncritically accept, the implications for their sense of self are immense. The girls in this interview, as well as the prior interview with Raven, Beverly, and Monica, show that they understand the need for their own internal control over how they display their bodies. In fact, Raven and Monica explicitly state that they should be trusted to exert this control and are angry at others trying to do so. Genevieve, too, sees that she can exert control over herself, but the motivation is quite different because it comes from outside, namely, from the kind of boy she hopes to one day marry and therefore does not want to tempt now.

9. Brumberg, *Body Project*, 97.

Lena is a 16 year old whom I met with in a restaurant over lunch. She is a Latina American girl whose parents and brother immigrated to the United States before she was born. When I asked her about temptation, she also brought up her body. Her response was a gesture toward her plate, which had a grilled cheese sandwich on it. She spoke with tears in her eyes about how food is a problem for her because she views herself as overweight. We had just finished talking about sin and evil, she was wrestling with trying to understand if there really was evil in the world, or if everything is relative. The example we talked about was Hitler. She wondered if he was in fact evil since it seems evil to kill so many people, but that he thought it was the right thing to do. She talked about how she herself has a "dark side" that shows up when she's in a bad mood, isolated, sad, or not her usual happy self around her friends. She said that evil is "usually what doesn't fit in society and rubs it the wrong way . . . Especially for girls who deal with it more, like society, for them being perfectly skinny so they have to probably bring out a side they wish they didn't or a darker side they wish they didn't, just to deal with those [expectations]." When I asked her about temptation, her answer was about food after talking about the relativity of evil and her times of depression,[10] which she had earlier related to talking about the expectation society places on girls to be "perfectly skinny." She said her sandwich was temptation because it was leading her away from healthy eating and losing weight, which she likened to a moral value. In this case, it seems that although she is not necessarily aware of it, society's pressure to be "perfectly skinny" has become a moral value, from which food is tempting her. Although she clearly sees the challenges with defining evil as relative, she seems to accept this definition of good from society, though she also seems to see that it is a complicated sense of good, since reaching that good requires girls to bring out their "dark side."

SIN

Related to the topic of temptation is the topic of sin. Although the girls I interviewed did not specifically say that temptation leads to sin, it seems a fair conclusion to draw based on what they did say. For example, Genevieve states that the boys in her youth group are trying to be "good Christians" but that girls make it hard (impossible?) for them to do so. The opposite of being a good Christian might be a Christian who sins, or yields to

10. My word, not hers.

temptation. Tay defines temptation quite succinctly as related to sin: temptation is "something that is guiding you more towards sinning than not sinning." Britt Nicole defines sin as "just deviating from God's desires for us as his children. . . . [I]t's an inescapable as human beings in general and you know, sin can be as big as murdering a person or as small as telling a lie. And, um, it's just anything that speaks less than God's name."

For most of the girls I spoke with, sin was a confusing topic. Brooke was recently grounded for sneaking into an "R" rated movie and her aunt wanted her to consider that Jesus would not have been happy with her watching that movie. She seemed unconvinced that this would be the case, which led her to define sin as something her aunt does not approve of. But she then went on to define sin differently for herself. She said, "But sin for me is like when I regret doing something. Like when I really want to do something and then I think back and I was like, 'Oh, I shouldn't have done that.' I think for me that's sin. And then, a lot of the times, I try to like twist my thinking like, oh well, I had to do that. I couldn't avoid it. So maybe it wasn't a sin . . . But whenever you twist your words, it's a sin." Most of the girls could not figure out how to define sin according to a list of dos and don'ts. They have received mixed messages about what a sin actually is and who gets to define it. Who gets to make up a rule about good Christian behavior anyway? Part of this is because girls trust themselves more than others do. Brooke was unconvinced that Jesus would care about her sneaking into an "R" rated movie, so she determined that sin meant something different to her aunt than it did to her. She takes her clues about sin from her own feelings around an action. If she feels bad, has regret, it was a sin. If she tries to convince herself that something was not really a sin, then it probably was.

Christian Smith and Melinda Lundquist Denton conclude that the dominant faith of teenagers in the United States can be termed "Moralistic Therapeutic Deism" (MTD).[11] This faith is evident in the way that many teenagers, religious and nonreligious, talk about their lives and their beliefs. One of the tenets of this faith, according to the authors who base their conclusion on thousands of hours of interviews with young people from all over the country, is that "central to living a good and happy life is being a good, moral person."[12] These morals can be provided by most of the world's religions, but are not dependent on them. They are general and broad and

11. Smith and Denton, *Soul Searching*, 162.
12. Ibid., 163.

subject to interpretation. "Being moral in this faith means being the kind of person that other people will like, fulfilling one's personal potential, and not being socially disruptive or interpersonally obnoxious."[13] For Christians, the language of something being "immoral" or "unethical" is usually something categorized as a sin. With this general definition of morality in the MTD faith of teenagers in this country, sin is therefore conceived of in incredibly broad terms, and it is relative, what is a sin to one person might not be a sin to another.

Many of the girls I interviewed struggle to understand what sin is because of this tendencies toward relativity on the matter. Their dissatisfaction with the definition of sin being so unclear comes from having been taught that sin is only something morally wrong. Moralisms are often a default for Christian teaching about sin—do this and it is good, do that and it is a sin. These moralisms do not engage the critical thinking that is emerging in this adolescent developmental stage. The girls I spoke with are smart and will not be satisfied with easy answers that do not engage their thinking. If they can argue their way around a moralism, then the topic a moralism seeks to counter—namely sin—loses credibility with them.

There were two girls with whom I spoke who did not only think of sin as a list of moralisms, Sadie and Tay. When I asked Sadie how she thought sin is, she defined it as "Something that drives a wedge between you and God." This is a very general definition and I pressed her for more detail. She clarified that she had learned in confirmation class that sin is "something that, like, separates you from God. I don't know, but it, it's like, it's, it's more comforting that way, because it's like, sin is not something that I am . . . " When it came to specifics about what it is that drives a wedge between a person and God, she does see room for relativity. "I feel like for some people, their phone might drive a wedge between them and God, but that's like for them. Some people it might not. Some people that's how they talk to people, and then God comes out of their talking, like I mean, I like that it's a personal thing, like, and it doesn't have to be a universal thing. Like for some people the fact that they have sex a lot could be a sin, or for some people it's like a celebration, I don't know."

The definition of sin as something that "drives a wedge between someone and God" is not like the other definitions I gathered from the interviews. This is a healthier definition for her because, as she says, sin is not who she is, instead it is something that separates her from God. In

13. Ibid.

Sadie's theology, God loves no matter what, and sin separates a person from the God who loves them. If instead, Sadie's theology was that sin is part of who she is, then it follows that she would have a hard time seeing herself as good or lovable.

Theologian Wendy Farley writes that traditional theologies of sin and atonement reinforce self-hatred.[14] Sadie seems to intuit this when she talks about her alternative definition of sin. In her definition, sin is outside of a person and causing a separation between that person and God. There is no need for self-hatred in her theology of sin because sin is not who she is. She finds this theology to be "comforting".

The discussion of sin came up in my conversation with Tay around a sermon she had preached a sermon at her church on the topic of teen cutting. She has friends who either used to or continue to cut themselves. Cutting is a form of self-injury that is quite prevalent especially among adolescents, and as of 2009, one study determined that girls were 3.4 times more likely to self-injure than were boys.[15] Self-injury is defined as "a behaviour that involves deliberately injuring one's own body, without suicidal intent and with or without pain," and cutting is the most common form of self-injury.[16] Tay is concerned about teen cutting and supports a nonprofit organization that works to prevent teen suicide and teen cutting; she also mentioned this organization in her sermon. She related that as a result of this sermon, she received "disapproving looks" from the people in her church. She says she would not feel comfortable bringing her friends to church because they, too, would be judged. Her church used to hear sermons that suicide is a sin. In fact, Tay has a friend whose grandmother is a member of her church. This friend's father killed himself, and the grandmother took her grandchildren, including Tay's friend, out of her will. Tay was not sure why the grandmother would do that, but she thinks it is connected with the idea that suicide is a sin. When I asked Tay if she considered herself a Christian, she said, "kinda" because her views about sin differ from her church's. However, when asked what her definition of sin is, she struggled to come up with a definition because she has been taught that suicide and gay marriage are sins but she doesn't believe that to be true.

On the one hand, Tay offered an image of sin as something that would make someone go to Hell if they did it too much. She said that she even

14. Farley, *Gathering Those Driven Away*, 163.
15. Duffy, "Self-Injury," 237–40.
16. Ibid.

pictures the devil with a chalkboard keeping track of everything someone does that is "against God's will." I asked her how she knows what God's will is, how she would know to avoid another tally mark on the chalkboard. She responded:

> I don't know, I think I always just like, pictured it in my own mind like, I always look at it on what God would think. Like, I don't think suicide is a sin because the people who are causing that person pain or *whatever is causing that person pain, I feel like that was the sin* and they just needed to get away with it and make sure that they were safe in their own mind. And, that things were OK. And that they could be with somebody who would care for them for eternity and not . . . treat them horribly like they were back down on Earth. And I feel like, like I, I don't know how to describe it, but um, I feel like a sin is something that God would not look past and be something that you wouldn't be able to get rid of if you did go to Heaven.[17]

Tay has two different concepts of sins. One shows a more traditional understanding that sin is something a person does. The image of the devil with the chalkboard keeping tally of things that "God would not look past" is stark and lacking in a theology of grace. The other is that sometimes there is something behind what a person does, which is the sin, rather than the action a person takes. For Tay, this concept of sin is at work in the situation of suicide. There is something behind the action of suicide, and that is sin. This concept of sin along with Sadie's understanding that sin is something that separates a person from God are the only two theologies of sin I heard in my interviews that were not focused on individual action or some unavoidable part of being human, or of being a girl whose body is a source of temptation for males.

A more common way the girls talked about sin can be seen in Sam's definition, "Uh, not following morals. Um, you know stealing and all that. I don't know if lying is necessarily sin. If it's, if it's a, if it's one of those helpful lies . . . I don't think having sex is a sin or having alcohol's a sin, or getting drunk is necessarily a sin. Because it's not really against a moral." Sam is unsure of what a sin is. She seems fairly confident that a sin is something that goes against morals, but she also seems unclear about what makes something a moral issue. "Stealing and all that" qualifies, but she can think of "helpful lies" and sees a hangover as a natural consequence of drinking too

17. Emphasis mine.

37

much rather than a sin that might have some spiritual consequence. When I asked how she came to believe this way about sin, she related it back to her theology, "You know, if God really forgives you on everything, why would God put you in Hell. You know? That's a really shitty punishment . . . Everyone, bad or good, deserves to go to Heaven. If they are forgiven. So, yeah."

Her theology consists of a God who loves and forgives. This is inconsistent with a God who issues eternal punishment for sin. She has not been taught, nor has she come up with, a theology of sin that is consistent with her theology about the nature of God. Her ability to see and point out inconsistencies between a more traditional understanding of sin and her understanding of God show that she is thinking deeply about her faith and trying to construct a theology without what she perceives as hypocrisy.

In one of the group interviews, this question of sin as relative came up and the girls discussed it together fruitfully. This part of the conversation includes Raven, Monica, Beverly, and Dawn. Dawn is a 17-year-old Caribbean American who lives with her mom and her brother. She and her brother were born in the United States, their mother was not. The girls were seriously talking about their understanding of sin, questioning and challenging each other, and engaging their religious formation with their experiences as they seek to determine a definition of sin in order to answer my question. Prior to this part of the interview, I had asked about their beliefs in God and sin had come up then as well. That part of the conversation set the stage for my specific question about sin. Monica began by suggesting that a sin is something that you know you shouldn't do but you do anyway. Beverly suggested that sin is a general category like murder, rather than something specific like don't get tattoos. Dawn then brought up the historical setting of the Bible saying that there are things prohibited in the Bible that just don't make sense in today's world. She also noted that sometimes it's more complicated than don't murder, because sometimes a person may be caught in a situation of kill or be killed. She concluded her thoughts by stating that, "it's a blurred line right now what sin is." Raven agreed, and added on to Dawn's historical reasoning by pointing out that it was men who wrote the Bible a long time ago. She made the comment that she gets confused about what is a sin and what isn't and that she had a conversation with her pastor about just that concern one day.[18] That conversation with

18. This is a wonderful example of an adult in Raven's church (her pastor) not avoiding relationship with a teenager, but instead making himself present and available to her as she struggled with her faith. When she spoke of the context of this conversation elsewhere, she noted that it happened when she was going through a hard time in her life

her pastor surprised her, and helped her to consider the historical setting of the Bible. Most surprising to her was that her pastor told her that he did not consider premarital sex to be a sin. When she considered the matter herself, however, she could think of reasons why it would be a sin, "'cause God made your, made you to be with a certain person I guess, so you're supposed to share that with one person. But then again, what if you fall in love with some person and marry that person, do whatever, people get divorced all the time. And then you marry someone else, or, you know, you do something else." She is confused and unsatisfied with her reasoning around sin. Is premarital sex a sin or not? What makes it a sin if it is one? Toward the end of this part of our conversation, Raven was pushing Monica on her idea that sin is something you do that you know you shouldn't do. She asked Monica if a sin is only a sin if it something is wrong under her own terms. Monica said yes, a sin is something you do even though you believe you're doing wrong. Raven countered, "Okay. Then what if you killed someone? And you wanted to believe that was right?" Raven draws the conversation out to its logical end. If doing something wrong is a sin, but different people think different things are wrong, then you can argue your way into never sinning by believing that everything you do is right for you.

These girls are trying to figure out if a sin is sin, or only if you know something is wrong and do it anyway. This part of the conversation ended with a discussion about how some people's religious values tell them to do things that are considered sinful to other people's religious beliefs. These girls seriously engage with the question about how to define sin and bring up reading the Bible as a document written within history and "by men" along with a conversation with a pastor. They do not come up with a definition of sin that is satisfying to the whole group, but they are critically thinking about it and wrestling with the implications of what it means if sin is relative. Perhaps Dawn said it most clearly when, at the beginning of this interchange, she stated that trying to define sin is confusing and a blurred line. These girls do not know what sin is. They are trying to synthesize what they have been taught, but are not coming up with any conclusions. The questions and the conversation, however, show keen interest and thoughtful engagement with the topic.

---

and pulling away from church. Taking seriously Raven's difficulties and interpreting her pulling away as contradictory to what her actual aims were, her pastor engaged her on her terms and took her seriously.

chapter 2

WAITING AND HOPING FOR
THE NEW CREATION

With the voices and stories of the adolescent girls in my head, some of which are presented in the previous chapter, I went to Paul's letter to the Roman Christians. I went to the scriptural text with the challenge that whatever it says must be good news to girls who had shared their struggles, their joys, and their gifts. I went with faith that Paul would have something to help the church fully embrace the gifts that these girls bring with them. I went knowing that his particular worldview had helped me understand my world and empower me as an active agent in it, and that he could offer something similar to these girls as well.

WHY PAUL?

The Bible is regarded as an authoritative source for ministry across the age spectrum in Christian churches. In my experience in churches, including their youth ministries, I hear Paul's epistles used in mainly moralistic ways: they are used to offer a black and white version of what a Christian should or should not do. They are used to explain the sinfulness of humanity as a result of human misdeeds. Paul's exhortative comments found in his letters are taken as isolated and conditional statements. Churches tend to use Paul to tell folks that if they do what Paul says, then they are really Christians (or really good Christians). His statements about sin are often interpreted as being the result of an individual's free will choosing (whether consciously or not) to act against God's will. He is often read as dualistic, seeing the body as problematic for the spiritual well-being of a person.

These interpretations of Paul are founded on a concept of the person as an individual who is willfully or ignorantly acting against God. The individual is charged then with making a decision to be better, to do better, and to stop sinning. This negative and individualistic view of the person in relation to God is then supported by interpretations that Paul provides people with the correct course of action, which although they are unable to take, should be aware of and feel badly about when they do not do so.

Paul's letters are rarely taught in churches in ways that offer liberation, despite Paul's own words declaring "For freedom Christ has set us free." (Gal 5:1a).[1] This word of freedom, a liberative word, in Paul's writings comes from his theological perspective on the world. In short, understanding Paul's worldview assists in recovering his writing as good news for Christians, and especially for adolescent girls. This is the Paul I met in that course in college. This is the Paul I heard as a resource to speak into the lived realities of the girls I met during the research for this book. This is the Paul the church needs to hear from, to teach, to preach, and to embody in its ministry.

Paul wrote that he received the gospel through a revelation from Christ. God has revealed the world for what it is through the act of Jesus as Christ on the cross. Paul says that the gospel was revealed to him (Gal 1:12). The Christ event—what happened on the cross when Jesus died and then was resurrected—reveals the identity of God and Jesus and also reveals that there are other players in the universe, namely the powers of Sin and Death. These "anti-God powers" were conquered in that event, though their presence is still very real in this time in between the Christ event and the "end times," the completion of the kin-dom of God.[2]

An important term Paul uses is "new creation." This is shorthand for both the new reality that is beginning since God has broken into the world as Jesus Christ and is also the term for the fulfillment of God's promise for which creation waits with longing (Romans 8:22–23). To know the world as Paul knows it is to see God's revelation in Christ, to perceive its effect on the whole of creation, and to realize that the powers of Sin and Death are defeated by Christ's death and resurrection.[3] Knowing from a new creation

1. All biblical citations are from the NRSV unless otherwise noted.

2. The term "anti-God powers" is from Martyn, "Epilogue," 179. Mujerista theologian Ada Maria Isasi-Diaz uses the term "kin-dom" instead of kingdom in order to reflect that God's vision is not patriarchal and hierarchal as the term "kingdom" connotes. I follow her in using the term in this book because it is inclusive and gender neutral.

3. Many New Testament scholars call this worldview of Paul's "apocalyptic" from his

perspective is to know the world and one's self through the new reality which Christ ushers in and in which Christians participate now through their incorporation into Christ through baptism. This happens in the present, though the new creation is not yet fully here. This is a typical way to talk about Paul's understanding of what time we are in—the already and the not yet. The kindom (or new creation in Paul's language) has begun already, but is also not yet fully here. In Romans 6, which will be explored in further detail in chapter 2, Paul writes that the life Christians live is lived in Christ's resurrected life. So Christians really do live in the new creation, and as new creations, while creation still waits for the new creation to be fully here for the whole of creation.

In this in between, or liminal, time, God's kindom that has begun is under attack. Looking at the promises of God for the world, one can quickly see that those promises and hopes are not yet fulfilled. This kindom, this new creation, just doesn't come in gently and begin a ripple effect of newness. This new creation comes in with a crucifixion. We are still on the other side of the resurrection and the world is still not as God hopes it to be. If God's sovereignty was unchallenged, the world would look quite different than it does. One New Testament scholar even calls the world a battlefield and likens everyone in the world to a soldier in the fight.[4] Another scholar, J. Louis Martyn, importantly points out that even though this is true, how the battle ends is not in question.[5] In the end, the new creation will fully come. Paul's perspective, that God's sovereignty is embattled, shows up in places like Romans 8:38–39 where the powers and principalities that threaten the Roman Christians are spoken of in stark language, though with the confi-

---

own use of the word. Paul believes the gospel to have been revealed to him in Galatians 1:12; the word is actually "apocalypsed" from the Greek. The term "apocalypse" has many connotations that are not what Paul (or these New Testament scholars) meant by the term. Beverly Gaventa, a New Testament scholar, understands the problematic nature of the term "apocalyptic." She rightly notes that often apocalypticism conjures images of violence, destruction, dualism, and escapism. See Gaventa, *Our Mother St. Paul*, 82–84. In the world of youth ministry, the term most likely brings up the *Left Behind* book series. This is not what Paul means by the term. Instead, there are several different traits of apocalyptic outlined and used by different scholars. Some of these traits are common across the work of several scholars including a concept of two aeons; the embattled sovereignty of God; cosmological language; an emphasis on suffering; and certainty of divine judgment of the present time. Apocalypticism has implications for how the individual is understood, for agency, and especially for the concept of Sin.

4. "[T]he world is not neutral ground; it is a battlefield, and everyone is a combatant." Käsemann, *Perspectives on Paul*, 23.

5. Martyn, *Theological Issues*, 64.

dence that they cannot separate "us" from the love of God in Christ. The powers of Sin and Death, which are the ones fighting against God are seen in Romans 5 and 6. The language of battle, war, and of Christians being enlisted as soldiers in this fight is powerful, although clearly violent.

Violence is not foreign to people in this country, and adolescent girls are no exception. Girls are aware of violence in this country. They have grown up in a post-September 11, 2001 world; they hardly remember a time when our country was not engaged in war. In the New York area, many were aware of the death rate of men of color in exchanges with police. Not only do they deal with this overt violence, but much of what they face is violence to their emotional and spiritual well-being. Stanley Coopersmith, educator and psychologist wrote, "Children return home from school each day like warriors home from the battlefield."[6] Although this language of war, battle, and soldiers must be examined closely and carefully, lest it seem Paul's theology encourages or celebrates violence, it is also true that it is an appropriate way to describe the lived experience of adolescent girls in our current time. In other words, it is not prescriptive, but it is descriptive.

Part of the reality and the difficulty of being in this battlefield of the in-between time, is that there will be suffering for those who are in Christ.[7] In Paul, passages about this suffering shows up often. This is the natural result of living at odds with the old creation by being part of the new creation in Christ. In Romans 8:18–19 Paul talks about how the sufferings of this age cannot be compared to the glory about to be revealed. In 1 Corinthians 4:13 he talks about how he is considered as refuse, which is proof of his being in Christ. For women and girls who suffer in some way, this can be good news: they can understand their suffering in a new theological way. However, like the language about violence and warfare, the idea of suffering as a new creation at odds with the old order must be handled carefully. Too many women and girls have stayed in abusive relationships because they feel they somehow deserve that kind of suffering. Debra W. Haffner has authored books on raising sexually healthy children and teenagers and is the founder and former director of the Religious Institute on Sexual

6. As quoted by Peck, "101 Ways to Fail School."

7. Susan Eastman notes that this kind of suffering is inevitable when one does not conform to, and even dies to, the old cosmos. See Eastman *Recovering Paul's Mother Tongue*, 109. She points specifically to Paul's labor pains in Galatians 4:19 and his call to the Galatians to become like him in Galatians 4:12. In fact, she notes that all the texts where Paul asks or tells his readers to become like him are connected to a "willingness to suffer for the sake of the gospel." See ibid., 28.

Morality, Justice, and Healing. She writes, "Dating violence is real. Almost half of girls *and* boys report that they have been hit, slapped, punched, or sexually coerced by their dating partner."[8] Too many girls have been told that "beauty is pain" as they starve themselves. There are also other ways adolescent girls suffer; some of those ways came up during the course of interviews for this project.

Paul offers an explanation and context for this kind of suffering. In his theology, the old age is marked by Sin being uncontested in its in control. So much so that it was able to even corrupt things that were very good, like the Jewish Law. In this in-between time, Sin still holds sway and causes suffering. Sin expresses itself in dating violence and the unattainable beauty myth.[9] Sin is found taking a foothold in relationships between people. A theology that takes Paul's perspective seriously exposes Sin for what it is and how it expresses itself in the lives of adolescent girls. This theology offers a way to understand why suffering occurs; it is at the hands of Sin. The present time is a time of suffering, and this suffering is temporary. And perhaps most importantly, Paul offers a theological context for suffering and a certain hope in its ending. He does not glorify suffering for its own sake and yet at the same time, he is also aware that suffering is inevitable in this in-between time.

For those who have been baptized into Christ, there is also hope at the present time because there is no such thing as suffering alone. Not only do they have people alongside them, the Body of Christ, while they suffer, their suffering is part of a bigger picture. All of creation is suffering because of the power of Sin. As girls cry out against injustice on a large scale and the intimate ways it affects their daily lives and concept of self, their cries join creation's own painful cries. Suffering does not happen for the sake of suffering; it occurs because it is part of waiting for the birth of the new creation. Moreover, in this time of suffering at the hands of Sin, girls are called to act against Sin along with other members of the Body of Christ. Those who are in Christ are told to fight against Sin. They do not sit idly by waiting for the new creation and hope they can endure the suffering long enough to see it come to fruition. They join forces with God against Sin and actively participate in the new creation's impending birth. They endure the suffering because it will assuredly end and because new creation cannot be birthed without it.

8. Haffner, *Beyond the Big Talk*, 151.
9. See Wolf, *Beauty Myth*.

Cosmological language is another marker of Pauls' writing. Paul writes in this way in places like 1Corinthians 15 and Romans 8.[10] There are actors in this world, more than just human ones. According to Martyn, these actors are God, humans, and anti-God powers. Sin is not only portrayed by Paul as the action of a competent human actor, but also as a supra-human actor itself. Moreover, the actions taken by these anti-God actors, which Paul calls "Flesh," "Sin," and "Death," are enslaving powers; they are against God and against freedom. According to this perspective, the Flesh as a power is not the same as a person's physical body, rather it is Sin establishing itself in a person, which includes their body, and commandeers human agency. Flesh becomes Sin's partner. In this way, whether one is "in flesh" or "in Christ," it is conceived of by Paul as a sphere of being, a world. This is dissimilar from typical body/soul or body/mind dualism. This is not about whether an individual decides that they are going to listen to their physical impulses or rise above them by means of spiritual fortitude. Instead, there are realms of power that exist because of the cosmological scope of the current time. The world of the Spirit of Christ invades the world in which humanity lives (where anti-God powers exist) and therefore humans can be ruled by the Spirit and fight against the anti-God powers of the Flesh while still in its corporeal reality. In the sphere of Christ, one is free, both bodily and spiritually, to operate differently in this world and be part of a new community that is not available when one is in the sphere of Sin.

Paul's theology is a way to conceive of the world, of time, and of reality as a whole. The claim of Paul is that this world, at this time, has been invaded by God in Christ. The anti-God powers Sin and Death still have power during this present time and are engaging in a war with the power of Christ and Grace and the Spirit. When this war is over, Grace will triumph. That outcome was decided in the resurrection of Christ. Those who are in Christ are living in the new creation already, while at the same time waiting for the new creation to come to its completion. They vicariously participate in the new creation through Christ's resurrection as they wait for their. This is a vivid and powerful way to conceive of reality. If taken as the true picture of the time in which we find ourselves, there are implications both for how to interpret Paul in the authoritative Scripture that is the guide of Christian faith and for how to live in this world. The implications for adolescent girls are powerful and exciting, including a new theology of Sin that speaks to

---

10. Martyn argues that Paul's apocalyptic is like the Hellenistic 3-Actor Moral Drama way of conceiving of the world. See "Epilogue," 177–78.

their experiences in a liberating way, including their understandings of the self, others, the world, and view of their bodies.

There are significant challenges to reading Paul in this way, because it is often so different from the traditional readings of Paul Christians expect. Paul is largely an untapped resource for liberative ministry for women, including adolescent girls. Certainly this in part due to the concerns feminist theologians, biblical scholars, and church goers have in struggling to find good news in texts like 1 Corinthians 14:34–35, where Paul writes that women should stay silent in church and submit to their husbands. These concerns are valid. Therefore, methods like biblical historical criticism should be brought to bear on interpretation of this and other problematic texts. Women who have been hurt by some of what is in Paul's letters and how these letters have been used by the church to oppress them will be surprised to find that Paul also offers the church a resource for liberation for women.[11]

Paul's letter to the Christians in Rome is different tone than his other letters.[12] In it, he is not responding to specific questions or concerns he has received about the community, nor is he building on his teaching in reference to specific situations of which he is aware in contexts with which he is intimately connected. This is a community he has actually not even visited. Romans addresses more general theological thoughts for a community with both Jew and Gentile members who share the same perspective on what has happened through the work of Christ on the cross and the implications of that event for life in their current time. In particular, chapters 6–8 of this letter offer a fruitful place to see how his worldview operates and to see why it can be helpful in ministry with adolescent girls. His attention to the body, sin, and the new creation in these chapters is particularly meaningful to the concerns and issues important to girls. In the course of these three chapters, Paul expresses clearly and with great emotion the heart of what

11. For example, Beverly Gaventa, writing about Galatians: "If instead of asking only about the relationship between Paul and the historical audience of this letter, or about Paul's attitude toward women, we ask about the letter's profound theological dynamics, then Galatians emerges as a powerful voice articulating God's new creation, a creation that liberates both women and men from their worlds of achievement and identity." See Gaventa, *Our Mother Saint Paul*, 74.

12. Paul does not use the term "Christian" to refer to members of communities who have been transformed by the gospel and believe in Jesus as Christ. Instead, he uses talks about these folks as being "in Christ" (for example, Romans 8:1). However, because "Christian" is the term generally used at present to describe these recipients of Paul's letter, I use it here. Elsewhere in the chapter I will also use "in Christ."

living in Christ can look like, the challenges of doing so, and the eagerness with which we wait for the New Creation.

ROMANS 6: WHAT IT MEANS TO BE IN THE BODY OF CHRIST

The term Paul uses for believers in the gospel is "in Christ." Paul begins chapter 6 by telling what baptism means, namely that people are completely united with Christ. In the church's current practice, baptism is a choice either made by parents/caregivers or by the person him or herself. Paul's language is different, however. He uses an interesting preposition in the Greek, meaning "into" Christ (v. 3). So people are baptized into Christ, which is why Christians are those who are "in Christ." A few verses later, in v. 8, he uses a different preposition for the participation in Christ's baptism, using instead the preposition meaning "with." Although these are little words, they carry a great deal of meaning for how we are to think of members of the Body of Christ. According to these verses, at baptism a person is drawn into Christ and with Christ in death and in life. The person has died and been buried with Christ. Christ was raised from burial by the glory of God. Because the believer is united with Christ in baptism, that person is living in the resurrected Christ.[13] Participation in Christ happens in a very real way at baptism for Paul. This participation means that one is living a new life in the present time. This new life is in Christ because Christ has already been resurrected and resurrection for believers is in the future. In some way, Christians are "walking dead" of the present time, animated by their being a part of Christ, who has been resurrected. Baptism is therefore not only a metaphoric or symbolic act with metaphoric or symbolic effects, it is also an actual way to participate, personally and communally, in concrete ways in what is happening cosmically and what has happened through God's action through Christ.

Using Janet Martin Soskice's religious metaphorical theory, Susan Eastman shows that metaphor is not something like frivolous language used for "emotional appeal." Rather metaphor is used to "describe reality in a way that the language of abstract thought cannot . . . [M]etaphors point beyond

---

13. Ernst Käsemann, in his *Commentary on Romans* writes, "Baptism is projection of the change of aeons into our personal existence, which for its part becomes a constant return to baptism to the extent that here dying with Christ establishes life with him and the dialectic of the two constitutes the signature of being in Christ," 163.

themselves to invisible realities."[14] Paul relies heavily on metaphors of death and life in this part of Romans to point to an invisible reality, namely that the life of the believer is completely different because of baptism.

Baptism here is not only symbolic death; it is actual death, co-death with Christ. This must be the case, because in the present age only actual death can completely sever the ties of Sin's control over a person. Only through Christ's death could Sin and Death be conquered. A believer's death in Christ through baptism severs Sin's complete control over that person. Dead in Christ and alive in Christ's resurrection means believers are able to live differently now while waiting for Sin's final and absolute demise. What dies in baptism is Sin's ability to imprison the believer's agency.

Baptism is not an action on the part of the Christian. Paul uses the passive voice, for example, "we were baptized" (v. 3), "we were buried" (v. 4), "we were crucified with" (v.6). Baptism happens to someone, as do the effects of baptism.[15] The life of the Christian is "seized" and becomes entwined with Christ's resurrected life in the present. The Christian's life is changed, and is now shared with Christ's life. The sharing happens mysteriously, and is possible because of the unique way that Paul views time.

Time is a strange thing for Paul. There are paradoxes to living in the new—but not completely new—time. "Eschatological reservation" is the term for what Paul does when he expresses that though death with Christ is possible now, future resurrection is not yet realized.[16] Though the work of Christ is a reality and participating in it (and its effects) is a reality, the end is not already here. Some things are reserved for the eschaton, the end time, including resurrection with Christ. His hearers therefore interpret their own existence in light of this liminal time. It is difficult to live as Paul exhorts them because the new creation is not yet here. And it is possible because they can live in Christ now.

One effect of baptism is that the believer has a new body; this must be the case since the old body has died with Christ. Paul calls this a "new mortal body." The believer has not physically died; that death is still in the person's future (as is that person's own resurrection). Metaphorically, however, that old body, which Paul calls "the body of sin," has died. This new

14. Eastman, *Paul's Mother Tongue*, 22.

15. Käsemann uses vivid language to describe this: "In baptism the new world initiated by Christ seizes the life of the individual Christian too, in such a way that the earthly path of the exalted Lord is to be traversed again in the life and Christ thus becomes the destiny of our life." *Romans*, 163.

16. Käsemann, *New Testament Questions of Today*, 132.

mortal is part of a new body (namely the Body of Christ, including both Christ's resurrected body and body of the Christian community). In fact, Paul's worldview seems to lack an idea of the autonomous individual; the individual is always connected to others and connected to either Sin or Grace.[17] "We share an old self with those who are under the power of Sin. Likewise, those who are baptized and are new, walk together in newness of life in Christ. This community with which they are united is not the same as the community of which they were a part under Sin. That old humanity has died, has even been co-crucified with Christ. This new mortal body is no longer a sinful body (part of a community under the power of Sin). However, because Sin still holds power in this time, even as a new mortal body, a believer is still susceptible to Sin's reigning in it (6:12).

Paul implores the community hearing his letter not to let Sin use their members as "weapons of unrighteousness."[18] Sin is so sneaky that it could come into even this Body of Christ and use part of it as a weapon against Grace. The community needs to actively guard against this. Paul holds believers accountable for this possibility. Using the imperative, he tells them not to present their members to Sin, rather present their members to God. Sin is opposite of and oppositional to God in this fight. Just as they are told *not to* present the members of their bodies so that Sin can use them

17. Paul writes that "our old humanity" (v. 6) has been crucified with Christ. This is a collective humanity. Paul uses the first person plural "our" with the singular word for "man" or "person." So, literally this means "our old person" but the sense of it can be "our old self." Käsemann makes this point about the lack of an autonomous individual as well. He writes, "our idea of identity is alien to the apostle's thinking," *Perspectives on Paul*, 10. Looking at Rom 6:12–14, he points out that the way that Paul talks about believers' bodies shows this non-autonomous anthropology. Individual Roman Christians are members of a community; having been freed from the body of death by dying in baptism, they are now members of the body of Christ. Käsemann writes that this means "that we are never autonomous, but always participate in a definite world and stand under lordship" of either Sin or Christ, though Christ is, what he calls the Christian's "true and only Lord," (*Romans*, 176).

18. Paul writes, *hopla adikias* in 6:13 which the NRSV translates as "instruments of wickedness." My translation "weapons of unrighteousness" shows more clearly Paul's theology that the present time is a time of conflict between Sin and God. Injustice or unrighteousness is a more accurate translation than "wickedness," in addition to showing the dichotomy that Paul sees between Sin and God, between righteousness and unrighteousness. The NRSV uses "righteousness" as a translation for *dikaiosynēs* later in the verse when translating Paul's imperative to the Roman believers to what they should do—present their members as weapons of righteousness. There is clearly the same root in those two words, which is why translating them similarly (unrighteousness, righteousness) also makes sense.

as weapons, they are told *to* present the members of their bodies to God so that God can use them as weapons of righteousness. Either way, these members will be used as weapons in the ongoing battle between Sin and God, between unrighteousness and righteousness.

For Christians now reading these words from Paul, we may well ask how it is that we are to make sure we are not being used by Sin. Is this a personal choice for the member? Is it the responsibility of the community of believers to keep its members from being used in this way? How does one know if they are being used by Sin or by God?

Käsemann sees that grace is the way for Christians to have the power to respond to Paul's imperatives to side with God. When one is under the power of Grace, one is able to "maintain the break with the world of Adam accomplished in baptism . . . "[19] This means that because of baptism, life in the present time happens through Christ, and the baptized operates under grace. All of this happens in community with other believers—one alone in Christ—and, in addition, a believer also experiences this new existence personally. Personally but not individually. As a believer experiences God's righteousness through their ability to respond to the call to act in concert with it, they are is also experiencing God.[20] Responding to a call to righteousness enables a believer to encounter the One who is righteous.

Because the future is not yet here, telling his hearers that they must live as if it is does not make sense unless they have the ability to do so. That ability comes not from their own force of will, but from the fact that their lives are connected with Christ's because they have been baptized into him. They are free to respond to the imperatives Paul places on them because they are free from the power of Sin. This does not mean, however, that it is always done. Paul would not warn his hearers of the possibility of still operating under Sin, even though they are baptized, if it were not possible.

These choices are how Paul express that there is an overlap between the old age and the new age in which a person now lives through his or her

---

19. *Romans*, 163.

20. To act ethically, or in concert with righteousness, for Paul is not about personal choice or making the right decisions, it is about living in the freedom of Christ in whom one is now living. Käsemann writes, "The premises are given in vv. 1–11, and vv. 12–23 make it clear that this freedom, grounded in the act of salvation and with baptism as the coming of the change of the aeons, can be maintained only in the practice of service. What is usually called ethics goes beyond the moral sphere, as certainly as it asserts itself in that sphere, because sin has moral implications of Paul even though it is not a moral phenomenon . . . [T]he Kyrios remains Kyrios only for the one who serves him." *Romans*, 117.

participation in Christ. Before baptism into Christ, there was no choice. The purpose of this crucifixion of the old humanity is "so that the body of sin might be destroyed, and we might no longer be enslaved to Sin. For whoever has died is freed from Sin" (6:6b–7).[21] The old humanity has been enslaved to the power of Sin. Because a new time began with Christ, baptized believers can participate in a new time and no longer need to be part of that old humanity that is the body of sin. Paul connects the power of Sin to the power of Death.[22] Because baptism is into Christ's death, Death no longer has dominion or lordship over that person, just as Death no longer had dominion over Christ once he died (see 6:9). The new body of this new humanity is a mortal body that is no longer under the lordship of Sin or Death and is no longer under law. Instead, this mortal body is under grace, walking in newness of life. The shape of this new life is still impacted by Sin.

Although it is true that one cannot become unbaptized, that one is no longer under the lordship of Sin and cannot fall back under that lordship once one is baptized, it is also true that while one lives in this present time, there is still the possibility of sinning, something against which believers must defend themselves. Although the hearers of the letter (and Paul himself) are under the lordship of Christ, eschatological reservation necessitates the possibility that they could *function* as if they still fall under the lordship of Sin. This is why Paul writes emphatically, using the imperative so often, in order to aid them in not doing so. Paul's forceful language is his way to help this not happen.

His metaphors not only point to a reality beyond the words themselves, but also operate to cause the hearers of the letter not to succumb to Sin's power now that they are free from it. Paul uses the metaphor of enslavement to Sin in vv. 6, 16, 17, and 20. He uses the metaphor of enslavement to righteousness in 16 and 18. In v. 22, he writes about being a slave of God. Being a slave to Sin, Paul says, keeps you free from righteousness but your *telos* (destiny) is death. A slave to righteousness, or to God, is freed from Sin and Death, and the *telos* is eternal life. The chapter ends with his

---

21. The NRSV does not capitalize "Sin" in these tho instances; however, it is clear that the way Paul is using the term here is as an actor and not as an action. In order to distinguish the "power of Sin" (the actor) from "sin" (an action), I opt for capitalizing the word.

22. Just as there is Sin the power and sin, what people do when they are under the power of Sin, there is also the power of Death, which leads to physical death. I use capital letters "S" and "D" when I am referring to the powers and "s" and "d" when referring to the human participation in those powers.

ARM IN ARM WITH ADOLESCENT GIRLS

statement, "For the wages of Sin is death, but the free gift of God is eternal life in Christ Jesus our Lord."[23]

The connection between death and Sin in this metaphor is also quite clear. Because alliance with Sin leads to death, when one is free from Sin, one is also free from the power of Death and does not die. Human death is the outcome, payment, or provision of Sin, but a believer has already died in baptism. This baptismal co-death with Christ operates quite differently because it leads to resurrection. The power of the finality of death is conquered through this act of incorporation into Christ. Sin and God/ Righteousness each offer something different for their slaves in exchange for their work as soldiers in the war they are waging against one another. The *telos* of being enslaved to Sin or a weapon of Sin in this conflict is death. But in baptism one dies, and yet does not die. Therefore the *telos* of enslavement to God or a weapon of God is eternal life. Importantly, this *telos* is a "free gift." It is grace, not payment or provision.[24] Neither Death nor Sin is the *telos* for those who have died with Christ. Therefore, since they have freedom from these forces, Paul entreats his hearers to choose to remain free from Sin and Death. There are consequences for this choice, no matter whose power one operates under, Sin or Christ.

The picture of how Christians can operate in the in-between time is both further explicated and complicated in the next chapter in Romans. Because death to Sin and Death has already taken place in baptism into Christ's death, but the resurrection into Christ's resurrection is still in the future, daily living now for those who are in Christ is difficult because Sin is still so powerful in the present. There exists the very real possibility that one who has been baptized can still fall on the side of Sin in his or her daily

23. This is another place in this chapter where the translation choices can make a big difference. Within the New Testament, this metaphor of the wages of sin is only found in Romans 6:23. In Romans 4:4, Paul talks about the wages due to a laborer and uses a different Greek word to express it: *misthos*. There is, therefore, a different sense of "wages" being used in this verse in chapter 6. The word used in the metaphor in 6:23, *opsōnia*, can also mean "provisions." In Latin, the word *obsonium*, related to the Greek, means "supplies and pay for an army" *An Intermediate Greek-English Lexicon*, 582. In this way, the wages of sin can also be linguistically connected to the provisions one needs in this war as a weapon of either Sin or Righteousness in the ongoing war between the two. Käsemann translates this word as wages being "soldier's pay" rather than some neutral compensation. Käsemann, *Romans*, 185.

24. Käsemann similarly points out that the construction is different for Paul between Sin and God. "Sin is already making the payment, death. The same image cannot be used for the God who gives . . . the comprehensive gift of salvation" *Romans*, 185.

living. The charge to act in concert with the lordship of Christ is real for those who are baptized. They represent Christ and show the world (including the power of Sin) that Christ has broken into it. Christians, then, are proof of Christ's salvific action in ushering in a new age.

ROMANS 7: LIVING IN/AS THE BODY OF CHRIST WHILE SIN IS STILL A THREAT

This next chapter in Romans shows Paul's struggle with what all believers struggle with—living according to the new creation when Sin is not yet fully defeated. 7:5 is one of the most emotional of Paul's writings. Based on the content of the letter up to this point and its most immediate context of Romans 6, I read Paul as writing honestly about his own current struggles to function in the present as one who is "in Christ" in this in-between time. The battle between Sin and Grace is enacted in his own body, while at the same time his body is a part of a new corporate body as the body of Christ. He writes honestly and emotionally about this struggle because of the potential for it to benefit the hearers of this letter. As Eastman points out, the function of this letter for Paul's audience is "a deepened personal recognition of both the horror of sin, and ultimately, the deliverance of God through the work of Christ."[25] Paul understands himself as an individual-in-relationship, both with Christ and with other believers. This relational existence comes through strongly in this section of Romans 7. Paul's emotional expression of the difficulty of living as one with Christ in this contested time is why this part of the letter is so powerful. The emotion comes through because it is autobiographical, even as the purpose behind it is clearly paradigmatic as he is teaching the Romans through this letter.[26]

25. Eastman, "Double Participation," 103.

26. Jewett recounts that there is an "immense scholarly debate" about Paul's switch to first person singular in this section of the letter, see *Romans*, 441. He lists some of the key scholars' interpretations in trying to determine whether, and in what context, Paul was writing autobiographically. Jewett himself sees Paul as writing "in character," rather than autobiographically. He writes that it is "artificially constructed in the light of his preconversion experience as a zealot, but with an eye to the current situation in the Roman churches." Ibid., 444. In other words, because of Paul's stated adherence to the Law ("blameless" he calls himself in Philippians 3:2) he cannot be writing autobiographically here since he is writing about ways in which he falls short of the law's expectations. He goes on to say that Paul's preconversion experience does provide evidence of sin in the form of zealotry as he expresses in Galatians 1:14. Ibid., 449. Käsemann argues that Paul is using this part of ch. 7 to offer himself as a paradigmatic figure. Paul, he says, is offering

Using himself as an example of how difficult it is to live into the freedom which the baptized have been given, he echoes the questions he asks in 6:1 and 6:15, asking again in 7:7, "What then should we say?" He uses these rhetorical questions to help the Romans see that they actually cannot draw the easiest conclusion from the situations he has presented. In this case, the simplest conclusion to draw is that if Sin and the law both bring death, we should see that the law is organically connected to Sin. But this is not where Paul goes. Only Sin is Sin; and it is powerful enough to even use the commandment of God toward an ungodly end (death).

Still, Paul goes on to say that the law is holy and the commandment is "holy and just and good" (v. 12). The nature of the law has not changed, but its purposes and effectiveness has been changed by Sin. He writes that Sin "seizing an opportunity in the commandment" (7:8) worked to bring death to him. Specifically, Sin finds this opportunity in Paul through the commandment against covetousness.[27] In this section of the letter, Paul is clearly writing with Sin as an agent of action. This makes clear just how powerful and manipulative Sin is in a way that Jews hearing the letter would have quickly understood. Sin even works through what is good to bring its goal of death to Paul. Sin is exposed by its working through the law. In fact, Sin is exposed for how utterly sinful it is.

In the latter half of ch. 7, vv. 14–25, Paul shares his ongoing struggle with Sin. Paul is in a state of confusion and frustration. He is unable to do the things he would like to do and does the things he does not want to do. In this part of ch. 7, Paul expresses with great emotion what it is like to operate as if one is under the power of Sin, when one's agency is directed

---

himself as an example of the failure of the religious or pious person to act in accordance with the will of God. Käsemann understands that Paul is writing this section using the first person singular as one who is "demonically enslaved," *Romans*, 204. Paul clearly expresses this stance, and is using not only the first person singular, but also the present tense. Therefore, I find it unconvincing that this section of Paul's letter (7:7–25) should be taken as only symbolically autobiographical or only referring to his life preconversion. Eastman asks the question of whether the identity of the first person singular in ch. 7 even matters. The point, she argues, is to express the struggle of the present time: "In other words, the speaker who talks as if he or she suffers under the tyranny of sin (and indeed, as if he were Paul himself) makes it possible to name a slippage between the cosmic, corporate realities of sin and grace and the discrete experiences of Paul's auditors. Naming that slippage prepares his auditors, in turn, to hear repeatedly and to appropriate personally the news of deliverance in chapter 8." "Double Participation," 102.

27. Käsemann argues that Paul chooses this particular sin because it is "absolutely the most basic sin against which the whole law is directed and which the law in fact provokes." *Romans*, 194.

by that power, even as one who has been baptized. He feels a distinct separation between himself and Sin, which does evil through him. It is not his own self doing evil, but Sin working through him, much like Sin works through the Law.

According to New Testament scholar Paul Meyer, Paul is writing about two aspects of the same self who is enslaved to Sin. "The symptom of this enslavement is not simple frustration of good intent, but good intention carried out and then surprised and dumbfounded by the evil it has produced, not despair but the same disillusionment so clearly described in v. 10: What should have effected life has produced death!"[28] The cosmic battle between Sin and Grace can be seen on smaller and much more personal scales—in God's good law and in one's self. Paul's purpose in writing this section of chapter 7 is to provide himself as a living example of what happens when one is under Sin. He knows this because he has lived it. Moreover, he uses the present tense; he is still living it. Though he has been baptized and is living a new life in Christ, so, too, is he struggling with the power of Sin still at work in the world and in his own life. Eastman says it clearly: "The battle is ongoing because, although those in Christ are no longer enslaved by sin, they still live in a cosmos dominated by sin and death."[29] So powerful is Sin that it can even try to enlist a baptized believer into its service.

In Paul's understanding, although there is a dimension of morality involved in what he writes about in vv. 13–25, it is not his primary concern. The emphasis is not on action, but rather his inability to act in a way that makes sense with his being in Christ. As Käsemann rightly points out, the situation Paul depicts of the pious is a desperate one.[30] One cannot do as one knows one ought, even when one is in Christ. What Paul offers then, is exactly the reason that the emphasis for living in Christ cannot be on the action of the believer who straddles these two worlds—the old and the new. The point is that when the emphasis or desire of the person is to be righteous rather than to be in Christ, then righteousness will not be the inevitable result. Sin cannot be conquered by the human drive to do good; Sin can only be conquered by Christ. Salvation is not an action of a pious human, it is an act of Christ.

The good news is that although Sin has found a way to work through Paul's body, Sin still cannot erase the fact that Paul is in Christ. The body

28. Meyer, "Worm at the Core of the Apple," 76.

29. Eastman, "Double Participation," 104.

30. Käsemann, *Romans*, 203.

is not bad, any more than the Law is bad. The body is not something to overcome or reject, but rather something that will be free and can even act in freedom now, though the war rages on.

This language of war and of Sin holding Paul captive through the members of his body echoes 6:12–14, with its military language and emphasis on the bodily experience of the believer. Paul sees that his own body is a dwelling place of Sin and is in need of deliverance even though he already has died in Christ. He has become a member of the corporate body of Christ who has been enlisted into Sin's army. His very flesh becomes a dwelling place for Sin when he no longer functions as free from the corporate sinful body. Sin is the reason why he does what he does not want to do and is unable to do what he does what to do. Importantly, it is not his own body or his flesh that is the problem, rather it is Sin dwelling in his members. This is also true of the corporate body—if Sin dwells in a member of the corporate body, it can turn the whole body into a weapon in the war against God. This is why it is the responsibility of the whole corporate body to help its members fight Sin and keep Sin from taking a foothold in it.

Because of this desperate position Paul is in, a cry for deliverance ushers forth. Chapter 7 ends with a desperate plea, recognizing Paul's own inability to wrest himself from Sin's grasp: "Wretched man that I am! Who will deliver me from this body of death? Thanks be to God through Jesus Christ our Lord! So then, with my mind I am a slave to the law of God, but with my flesh I am a slave to the law of sin" (7:24–25).

Paul is certain that both he and the Romans listeners are dependent on Christ for salvation from their predicament. His soteriology does not include pitting will against action in 7:14–20, as some might deduce. The contradiction does not fall on the moral plane. Instead it is that the pious person thinks he or she can act in such a way as to attain salvation on their own. Of course this is impossible, as salvation cannot come from anyone or anything other than Christ.[31] Even in this state, Christ saves. Thanks be to God!

Deliverance from this body of death will come through Jesus Christ. Deliverance from being aligned with Sin, and realignment with Grace will come through Jesus Christ. Here, Paul changes the tense again. Although he uses the present tense to show that the struggle is taking place even though he is a baptized believer, deliverance is still in the future. Deliverance will be complete. On a personal level, because Paul is in Christ, he

---

31. Käsemann calls this the "heart of Paul's teaching," *Romans*, 209.

is aware of the ways that Sin is attempting and sometimes succeeding in gaining a foothold in his own body. On a communal level, Paul's personal awareness is paradigmatic: because the Romans Christians are together in Christ, they can perceive when Sin is taking a foothold in their corporate body. On a cosmic level Sin has been defeated, so the conflict is now only relegated to these personal and communal levels.[32] The future promise of deliverance, or rescue, from this "body of death" is a certainty like participation in Christ's resurrection.

ROMANS 8: LIVING IN CHRIST WHILE WAITING IN HOPE

When Paul moves into ch. 8, he begins with an incredibly hopeful statement for those who are caught in this struggle between Sin and Righteousness that he has just described in ch. 7. He writes, "There is therefore now no condemnation for those who are in Christ Jesus." Although Sin is dwelling within the members of a baptized person and causing the person act in such a way that is inconsistent with living in Christ, there is no condemnation. The struggle with the effect of Sin's power is clearly felt in the turmoil expressed in the previous chapter. But there is no condemnation. The "body of death" Paul expresses in the previous chapter is not where humans stay, rather they are saved and brought into newness of Spirit. Although the baptized person's resurrection into Christ's resurrection is in the future, the present is not a place of condemnation or death, but a place of life. The believer does not lose their place in Christ, their membership in the Body remains.

Käsemann helpfully summarizes this chapter like this: "[v]erses 1-11 deal with the Christian life as being in the Spirit. Verses 12-17 expound this as the state of [adoption as children]. Verses 18-30 portray it as the hope of eschatological freedom. Verses 31-39 depict it as triumph."[33] This description of the Christian life, what it involves, and the result of living it will

32. Eastman terms the life of the believer as "double participation." She writes, "On the one hand, the objective redemption accomplished by Christ's action on the cross is sure, and the victory is accomplished (8:3). On the other hand, continued vulnerability to the powers of sin and death, entailing—this side of the eschaton—a life of double participation." Eastman, "Double Participation," 107.

33. Käsemann, *Romans*, 212. He uses the term "sonship" in talking about verse 15, from the Greek word *uiothesias*. Along with the NRSV translation, I am choosing to use "adoption" here as a gender neutral term.

conclude my close examination of this part of Romans for the purposes of ministry with adolescent girls. The description of the challenges, triumphs, and relational nature of life in Christ will be explored in this section.

Jewett points out that because of the strength of Paul's argument in ch. 7 where he "so eloquently and terribly portrayed" the "paralysis caused by the reign of sin," he must be equally forceful in his expression of the new age in which believers now operate.[34] This force is expressed through law. In vv. 2 and 3, there are different laws—the law of the Spirit of life in Christ Jesus, the law of Sin and Death, and the law (Torah) which has been weakened by the flesh.[35] Those who are in Christ are free from the law of Sin and Death and the law weakened by flesh (Torah) because of the law of the Spirit of life in Christ Jesus. Freedom from the old age is freedom from these old ruling categories, and freedom for the law of the Spirit of life in Christ. Being in Christ means being in relationship with a new law; this time it is one that leads to life.

One of the most important interpretative moves for ministry with adolescent girls comes in right here. Paul writes a lot about flesh in this first part of ch. 8. The girls with whom I spoke are well-acquainted with theology that comes from one interpretation of Paul's use of the term. This interpretation is that the body is sinful; it must be covered and overcome in order to have a fruitful spiritual life. However, another interpretation is possible, and more faithful to Paul's worldview. When Paul uses the term "flesh," it is shorthand for the human, and for humanity, under Sin. Human flesh, the body, is not inherently sinful; the problem is not with the flesh, the problem is that Sin can manifest in the flesh and can in fact create a corporate body of death, made up of members of death.[36] Those who are in

---

34. Jewett, *Romans*, 480.

35. Jewett, tracing scholarly debates, points out that there is not agreement about whether there are three different laws being discussed in these verses. Paul could be equating "the law" in verse 3 with the "law of sin and death" in verse 2, meaning he is only talking about 2 laws, one of which is the law of sin and death (and is also Torah). It is my contention that there are three laws: 1) the law of sin and death, 2) the law (Torah), and 3) the law of the Spirit of life in Christ Jesus. The law of sin and death is certainly at work in the Torah. This is what Paul writes about in chapter 7; however, he does not equate Torah with Sin. By no means! Jewett argues that there are two laws: 1) The law of the Spirit of life in Christ Jesus and 2) the law of sin and death. In both cases, the Torah is at play. In Christ, Torah is the law of the Spirit of life. Under Sin, Torah is the law of sin and death. Since Paul does not expect believers to follow Torah, I find it unlikely that he is writing about the law of the Spirit of life in Christ being Torah. *Romans*, 481.

36. This language comes from Romans 7:24.

the Body of Christ are rescued from being a part of humanity under Sin. Those who are in the body of death are the ones whom Christ comes to rescue by incorporating them into his body of resurrected life.

Because Sin has exercised its power over people and the law, God did something different; God sent someone to do what the law could not. Paul writes that God sent God's son in the "likeness of sinful flesh" (8:3). Only then can Jesus complete the task of condemning Sin as it manifests itself in flesh. Some people wonder if this phrase of Paul's means that Jesus was in some way not really human; was he only human-like? Understanding Paul's worldview here helps to figure out what he means. Jesus is both like and unlike humanity. He is "in the likeness" of humanity under Sin; but unlike humanity under Sin, Jesus is instead under the power of Grace. In this likeness, Jesus is able to claim humanity for Grace against Sin. Humans are able, in a way that they were not able when there was only the law (because Sin found a way to use even that), to live as part of a body that is free from Sin. Flesh under Sin is what Jesus condemns when he himself is in the likeness of that sinful flesh. Jesus does not condemn human flesh, but the Sin which has taken over flesh and has become its descriptor. Just as in ch. 7, Paul is talking on different levels. On one level, there is the individual, who is always in relationship with other people and with either Sin or Grace. On another level, there is the corporate body of believers who together participate in this place and time as the body of Christ. On yet another level, there is a corporate body to which an individual belongs when Sin has made use of that member's body—the body of death. Paul is always talking to the individual-in-relationship and the body to which that individual belongs. Both the individual-in-relationship and the body of death are rescued and transformed when Sin is defeated. There is no condemnation for those who are in Christ, because Christ is the one who does the condemning. What he condemns is not people who have died and will be raised with him, but Sin itself.

Here in ch. 8, Paul further describes the new life for those living in Christ. He explains that this is new life in the Spirit and is righteousness (v. 10). How one lives and walks in their life has a great deal to do with where their mind is directed (vv. 5–7). There is both a moral component and spiritual component to what it looks like in the concrete lives of believers. The Spirit is linked with God, righteousness, Christ, life, and peace. People participate in the conflict between Sin and God as they walk according to one or the other. The conflict is not an inner conflict relegated to the individual between someone's body and spirit or soul. The conflict is much larger; it is both communal and cosmic in scope. What is at stake is resurrection, life in the present, and life in the future age to come as well.

Paul has written that those who are in the flesh do not have the power to please God. But, those hearing this letter ("you") are not in the flesh; they are in the Spirit because they are in Christ. Baptized into Christ means that "the Spirit of God dwells in [them]" (v. 9). Jewett translates the "in" in v. 9 as "within" or "in the midst of" to aid in conveying Paul's corporate meaning. God's Spirit dwells evn "the congregation, rather than merely within the heart of individuals."[37] Individuals are baptized into a community of other Christians and into the body of Christ. There is a both/and sense to this indwelling Spirit; it is within individuals-in-relationship, and it is in the midst of that community. The truth is that when one is dwelling in the Spirit, the Spirit also dwells in him or her, and the result is life. This is not some spiritual, disembodied life, it is bodily life.[38]

Those who "walk according to the Spirit" in this liminal time, are those who are adopted into the lineage of Christ. In v. 15, Paul shows what enslavement to the Spirit (7:6) looks like. It does not look like slavery; it looks like adoption. Käsemann helpfully connects Paul's idea of slavery and adoption: "Radical obedience is pointedly defined as slavery. But . . . it also denotes genuine freedom and [adoption as children]."[39] He writes that we (Paul and the believers in Rome) cry out to God as a parent and are ourselves children of God and heirs of God along with Christ. This cry comes not from the individual alone deciding to cry out to God, but instead it comes from the Spirit bearing witness to who God is, along with and

---

37. Jewett, *Romans*, 489.

38. Using "flesh" (*sarx*) until now, Paul now writes about the body (*sōma*) in verses 10 and 11. Flesh is characterized as another power, something put in the service of Sin by Sin. To live according to the flesh finds expression in the body. Interestingly, death of the body is on both sides of the battle. Because of Christ's own death and because of baptism, even on the side of righteousness bodily death and participation in Christ's death is a reality. The bodies of these Romans have died with Christ just as Jesus' body died because of the power of Sin; it is just these dead mortal bodies which are promised to be brought to life through Christ's spirit. Jewett connects the body of death, *sōma nekron*, in v. 10 with the body of sin, *sōma hamartias*, in 6:6, which occurs during Paul's discourse on baptism (*Romans*, 491). In that section the body of sin is co-crucified with Christ, putting it to death for the purposes of life. In this instance in vv. 10 and 11, something similar is happening. Echoing baptism, here in ch. 8 the body of death is put to death for the purposes of life. Sin and Death are again linked for Paul, and are linked in the bodies of humans.

39. Käsemann, *Romans*, 227.

within the spirit of the people. This is clearly a dance of cooperative agency. The Spirit is cooperating with these people and bearing witness to God with their spirit. Here Paul is using the singular, "spirit," as he does in verse 10. The spirit with which the Spirit is bearing witness to God is a shared communal spirit of these people. Though they have separate mortal bodies, these children and heirs of God are of one spirit.

Being sisters and brothers of Christ (co-heirs) is not an easy way to live in this contested time. Suffering is a reality for those who live in a way that conflicts with the power of Sin. Suffering and dying with Christ is part of being in Christ and having the Spirit dwell within. Resurrection cannot happen without death, neither can glorification happen without suffering. This is what it means to live in the world where Sin and Death are exercising their power over and against the power of God. To be sure, suffering is also part of being enlisted on the side of Sin in this conflict; suffering with Christ, however, is different suffering. Just as dying in Christ is different than physically dying.

Suffering in Christ is contextualized, temporary, and never justified. Suffering happens in a conflict, such as the one between Sin and Grace. When a war raging, there are injuries for those on the battlefield, which is where all people are located. When one is in Christ, suffering gets exposed as part of Sin's battle plan. Suffering is not glorified or sought after; rather it is a sign of Sin's continuing, yet passing, power. Although suffering must be endured, it is not embraced. Paul then goes on to say, that although suffering of the present time is connected with the glory that is to come, these two (suffering and glorification) do not have the same value; they cannot be compared (v. 18). It is not the case that suffering does not matter. Indeed suffering shows the power of Sin at work so it matters a great deal. Suffering can also show that a believer is living according to the Spirit, therefore caught in the conflict between Sin and Grace. In any case, present suffering is not congruous with the glory that will be revealed to or among us. Paul assumes that all believers will suffer; this is a mark of the present age. Suffering is not, however, the only mark of the time. The time is also marked by the promise of glory, which will be revealed. This glory is something for which all of creation is waiting. According to Jewett, the Christian community in Rome is the "initial evidence" of the glory that is coming for all creation.[40] They have a hint of the fulfillment of the promise in their own gathering, even as together they see that the present time is one of suffering.

40. Jewett, *Romans*, 511.

What creation is waiting for is not resurrection or glory or even the revealing of Christ. Creation is waiting for the revealing of the heirs of God. As Jewett says, "Paul implies that the entire creation waits with baited breath for the emergence and empowerment of those who will take responsibility for its restoration, small groups of *huioi tou theou* [sic] ("sons of God")."[41] As the heirs of God wait for glory and an end to suffering, and for participation in Christ's resurrection, creation is waiting for them. The responsibility of the heirs of God to their world is clear. There is no denial of creation or escapism in Paul's worldview. Instead, Paul helps the believers in Rome realize that when they participate in the death and resurrection of Christ, they become what creation is longing for.

Creation is in the position of longing for this revelation because it has been "subjected to its futility" (v. 20), unable to set itself free from its "slavery to destruction" (v. 21). Creation's problems are the result of human arrogant and selfish pursuits.[42] Yet creation is waiting for its freedom to come from humans, specifically humans who are heirs of God. Creation is waiting for those who cry out to God, those who are hearing Paul's letter. Creation cannot free itself; its subjugation was not accepted willingly and did not happen by its own will. Paul understands that creation's subjugation to its futility was done "by the one who subjected it in hope" (v. 20).[43] God seeks freedom for all, which is not something creation (including the people in it) can achieve for themselves. Freedom comes through Christ, it is both accomplished in his resurrection (and therefore Sin's inability to work death in Christ) and is something for which creation (and the people in it) are still waiting.

---

41. Ibid., 512.

42. Jewett understands that Paul is connecting creation's yearning to the biblical tradition in what Christians call the Old Testament. He finds parallels to what Paul is writing about in Genesis, Psalms, and Ecclesiastes (*Romans*, 513). Jewett sees Paul pointing out the responsibility humans bear for the abuse the natural world has endured (*Romans*, 513). He notes that "[w]ith such clear allusions to this biblical tradition, Paul's audience could well have thought about how imperial ambitions, military conflicts, and economic exploitation had led to the erosion of the natural environment throughout the Mediterranean world, leaving ruined cities, depleted fields, deforested mountains, and polluted streams as evidence of this universal human vanity" (*Romans*, 513).

43. This statement is a challenging one, putting God as the agent who does the subjugating. Theologically, this is necessary, God must be the one subjugating creation, because otherwise Sin is stronger than God. For Paul, the purpose of God doing so is for the purposes of freedom and salvation. Käsemann points out that this verse is in anticipation of 11:32 where "all are held under disobedience in order that mercy may be shown to all." Käsemann, *Romans*, 236.

The promise of that freedom from bondage to destruction (or to Sin and Death) is something Paul says "we" wait for with patience and hope. Creation waits. We wait; not only with patience and hope, but also with groaning, as a woman in childbirth (v. 22). This groaning happens collectively as well. Creation is groaning together; and we are groaning with creation. As we are saved in Christ, we are also saved in hope. Christian hope, then, is an essential part of living in the liminal space of this contested time. The pains of a woman in childbirth are severe; they are also temporary and for the purpose of new life, something wonderful. Christian hope, the hope of creation and of humans, is hope for this suffering to end with the gift of new life. This hope is for the "redemption of our bodies" (v. 23), not the redemption of the soul separate from the body, but the redemption of the body. Resurrection for Paul is bodily because he does not have a dualistic anthropology. For Paul, both redemption and resurrection are embodied realities for which humans hope.

In this place of waiting and patience for redemption, resurrection, and freedom, Paul notes that we do not wait alone. In our weakness or infirmity, the Spirit comes alongside us with help (v. 26). Jewett writes that the implication is that the Spirit "stands alongside the saints as they persevere, guiding their most decisive intervention into the fallen world, namely, their prayer."[44] Just as in verse 16, the Spirit does not work alone, nor do the believers. The help is cooperative, the Spirit helps alongside the weak person. The translation used by the NRSV is "the Spirit helps us in our weakness;" it is important to be clear that this help is not the surrender of the person's agency to a Spirit who can fix something in our stead, but rather a cooperative partnership. The Spirit helps with us.[45]

This help is needed because "we do not know how to pray as we ought." In this liminal time when we seek to be patient and wait with hope for redemption, Paul knows that prayer is needed. This prayer is aided by the Spirit's intercession. The Spirit itself intercedes for us with "groans not expressed in words" (v 26). These groans echo the groans of creation waiting in pain like that of childbirth, Paul uses the same root word for both in verse 22 and in 26. The Spirit's intersession happens "on behalf of saints according to God" (v. 27). When the person is unable to participate in this

---

44. Jewett, *Romans*, 521.

45. Paul uses the prefix *syn-* along with the parsed form of the verb *antilambanō*, which means "to help." With the prefix *syn-* Paul makes clear that this help is not from outside the person with no interaction with that person.

cooperative dance, the Spirit steps in to intercede, as is God's will. Even in this situation, however, it is not the absence of the person that enables this intercession. God does not eliminate human agency, rather the Spirit enhances it. Even in a state when the person cannot pray, the heart of the person is connected with the Spirit. Paul writes that God "who searches the hearts, knows what is the mind of the Spirit" because of this intercession.[46] Now we also learn that the hearts of the people are connected to the mind of the Spirit. The Spirit's intercession in times of weakness is God's design. We also learn in this verse that these people in this cooperative dance with the Spirit are holy; they are saints! Paul does not say that they are holy once they are no longer weak; rather, these people are holy in their weakness as the Spirit intercedes for them.

The end of ch. 8 is encouraging for Paul's audience. He writes of Christ interceding for us (v. 34) in the same way that he wrote in vv. 26 and 27 about the Spirit interceding. In vv. 35–39 Paul makes a list of challenges that could "separate us from the love of Christ," and then states with certainty that "in all these things we are more than conquerors through the one who loved us" (v. 37). We cannot be separated from the love of Christ because it is through that very One that all these things are conquered.

We are conquerors in the present because of Christ loving us in the past. Salvation does not happen through human will or action. Moreover, conquering does not happen through an act of violence or forceful subjugation, instead it happens through love. Jewett writes, "[t]his supervictory therefore derives not from the skill and strategy of combatants but from the power of the gospel, which declares the love of God shown on the cross of Christ."[47] Paul presents the paradox of new creation in these verses of triumph.

SUMMARY

These three chapters show, in a pretty concise way, key parts of Paul's theology and worldview. In these chapters readers hear about what it means to be in the Body of Christ in this liminal and contested time. Baptism is explained as incorporation into Christ's death and resurrection, thus breaking the power of Sin's hold on this individual-in-community/-in-Christ. Paul then shares with the Roman believers that living in Christ does not

46. My translation of Romans 8:27.

47. Jewett, *Romans*, 549.

completely shield a believer from the reach of Sin. Instead, he takes seriously the struggle of the believer to act in a way that is consistent with his or her participation in the resurrected life of Christ because Sin is so strong. Paul uses himself as an example, showing his hearers that he is in the same struggle that they are to act through Christ and not captive to Sin. He ends ch. 7 with the certainty of salvation and gratitude for Christ's ongoing work. Then Paul explains what it means to live in the Spirit and about what will come next; the new creation is fully here and the present contested age gone. The promise of new life of freedom from Sin is for all creation. Creation waits patiently with hope because this promise *will* be fulfilled, without a doubt. Paul understands the pain of the present time and does not attempt to justify it, only to proclaim that it is temporary and in fact a sign that Sin's power is going to end.

From these important, descriptive, and powerful chapters, the church has much to consider. In them is the possibility of a new way to interpret the world, the time, itself, the church's call to action in the world, and the members who comprise it.

chapter 3

PAULINE THEOLOGY FOR ADOLESCENT GIRLS

After closely reading Romans 6–8 and listening closely to girls' stories and experiences, I can see several particular places where Paul's theology can offer a helpful and liberative lens to girls seeking to understand and interpret their lives.

THE NEW MORTAL BODY

In offering adolescent girls a theology of the body that describes the body as good, but with caveats that imply instead it is dangerous and shameful, the church denies young women the opportunity to be in right relationship, through their embodied selves, with themselves, others, and with God. A theology of the body that instead values the body as sacred and honors all the messy realness of embodiment is aware that the body is the primary way girls relate to their world, the people in it, and God. Developing this kind of theology with adolescent girls is an essential, yet often unrealized, task of ministry with girls. A theology of the body like this provides girls, and the church, with the possibility of liberation from damaging societal pressures, assumptions, and expectations around the female body. It also offers girls an opportunity to practice justice-making, because this theology of the body is necessarily active. This is exactly the kind of theology that can be developed through deep interactions with Paul's writing.

In Romans 6, Paul writes about the body within the context of baptism, life, and death. Paul, too, values the human body. It is an important part of our connection to and participation in Christ. A believer is in a new and different state having died (and died to death) and now being alive in Christ. This is not an overly-spiritualized state of being alive, but rather an embodied, mortal state of being alive in Christ. Paul offers an imperative for believers to not allow their bodies to be weapons of Sin and to instead present their bodies (of members [of the body] to God). In traditional theologies of body offered to adolescent girls, this may be interpreted as keeping the body pure, apart from other bodies, and clothed conservatively so that it is acceptable to God. Essentially, girls are told to keep their bodies as spiritualized as possible, to refrain from their bodies looking and acting like bodies. Paul offers something different. Moreover, the goodness of the human body is not only established at creation with the *imago dei,* but in the fact that Jesus Christ himself was embodied. This incarnational theology is what makes Christianity so effective when talking about the body.

In this liminal space and time, Paul says that our bodies, our mortal bodies, are part of the conflict of the age. They can be used by Sin, or they can be used by God. It is not by denying or overcoming embodiment that bodies can be used by God. Our bodies, as bodies, can be instruments for defeating Sin when they are in service to God. Through God's grace, the believer can offer their body to God. Grace operates as a power that breaks the power of Sin. Christ comes in the likeness of sinful flesh, dies, and is resurrected bodily. Through baptism, believers, too, experience death of their association with Sin and life in the present in bodies that can now work together with God for the purposes of freedom in this contested time. What this looks like for adolescent girls has something to do with power. Power is a key part of how Paul sees the world. The power of Christ overcomes the power of Sin. Although the present is still a contested time, the future is assured—final and complete power of Christ and Sin's ultimate demise.

Paul is often seen as the biblical justification for dualism between the body and the soul or spirit. In Romans 6–8, there are certainly instances that can be read as dualistic, and inherently anti-body, if not read with awareness of Paul's worldview. In Romans 6:6, Paul writes about the death of the "body of sin" as the way to no longer be enslaved to the power of Sin. He states that having been baptized, the believer is alive in Christ, under the power of grace, and enslaved to God, who is righteous. His writing can be interpreted as saying that one's body must be subjugated in order to allow a person's sinful body to be overcome by grace. Accordingly, when Paul writes that believers must not allow their members to be used by Sin but instead be used by God, righteousness is then interpreted as denying some parts of the body or some functions of the body so that the person is righteous like God is righteous. Youth ministries find fodder here for teaching moralisms and condemning certain practices of the body: Don't have sex. Don't smoke. Don't drink. Don't reveal too much skin. These activities show that you are still in your sinful body. Righteous bodies don't do these things; and the impulses to do these things come from the body and must be controlled or ignored. What girls need is a theology of body that honors the complexities in which girls (and, indeed, all of us) live and heals them of the shame they have be taught about their bodies and about sexual desire.

Understanding Paul's perspective on the world yields an interpretation of these texts about body that can be the foundation on which to build a healthy theology of body. In baptism, the believer's body no longer falls under the power of Sin (is no longer a member of the body of Sin, but rather is a member of the body of Christ, to use language from 1 Corinthians 12). Dualism is not between body and soul; it is between Sin and God. To be alive under the power of Grace changes the way the individual's body relates to the bodies of others. In fact, the individual is alive in Christ's own body. A believer's body is a place of redemption and life. To be implored not to present one's body to the power of Sin does not boil down to a list of dos and don'ts. Instead, it is to understand that one's life, including one's body, operates in a new and different space. A space of life, power, and freedom. In that space, dos and don'ts mean very little.

Moreover, the admonition is to the body of believers to not let Sin take away one of the members of that corporate body. Paul is concerned that the body of believers take care of one another and make certain that Sin is not trying to pry someone away for its own purposes against the Body of Christ. What matters is a larger question of relating to others, oneself, and God in a way that reflects one's position under Grace. Adolescent girls can find help in interpreting their relationships and in constructing new relationships in their Christian communities. This happens when these communities practice their faith by seeing the body as a "site and mediation of divine revelation" as M. Shawn Copeland calls it.[1] However, this is not how girls understand their bodies according to their faith communities' explicit and implicit teaching.

---

1. Copeland, *Enfleshing Freedom*, 2.

The way Raven describes how her body is discussed to by others shows overt racism, sexism, and sizism. Monica also points out the explicit sexism she experiences in her church. The message these girls receive is that despite the fact that they are believers, their bodies are viewed as sinful and tempting to men. Their bodies are problematic to the spiritual lives of men because their bodies are female. They interpret these messages as coming from men, rather than from God. They do not feel condemned by God, but rather by their church and by other Christian believers. They are frustrated and angry about this, yet feel powerless to do anything about it. Several of the girls from another of the group interviews, noted similar expectations for girls to choose their clothing in order to avoid tempting boys. Tay has been taught that her body is less valuable, less important, and less desirable than a skinny body. The church is at least complicit in this value system, as they have offered her nothing to counter it.

Girls receive similar messages about their bodies at church and at school. From Sadie who reports feeling fat because of other kids asking her about her weight and wanting to have input into where she buys jeans, to Sam who feels she was put up for adoption because of her female body, to Raven and Monica who get told explicitly by folks in their church that they reveal too much skin, to Genevieve and Britt Nicole who see the female body as tempting boys away from being good Christians, the message that bodies are dangerous and even sinful and that only certain bodies are acceptable and valuable is heard and sometimes uncritically accepted by these girls. Many of them feel that some changes need to happen to their bodies in order for them to be accepted by adults, their churches, their friends, or themselves. None of them discuss their bodies in positive ways. None of them have received empowering messages from their churches about their bodies. None of them have been taught that their bodies are how they relate to God. They only receive messages that interpret their bodies as under the category of sin, rather than grace.

The teenage body is powerful. Physical and physiological changes happen at a rapid rate. Parents, ministers, and other caring adults are understandably often fearful that these new hormones, sexually mature bodies, and lack of impulse control will lead to sexual activity that can damage a teenager emotionally, psychologically, and physically. Sexually transmitted infections and diseases and the rates of teen pregnancies are significant reasons why teenagers should be taught about the possible consequences of sexual activity. In one conversation with a group of adolescent girls in my own ministry, I asked what they were taught in sex education in school. They relayed that they were taught that sex is scary. The focus of their public school education was on the consequences of sex, emotionally and physically. They told me they felt they were led to believe that sex ultimately leads to death. This conversation took place in the early 2000s. The over-sexualization of female adolescent bodies is damaging to girls' sense of themselves and distorts how adults and peers relate to girls. The theological solution, however, is not to condemn the body as sinful and caution against its poisoning the otherwise pure soul of adolescent girls. Instead, using Paul's worldview of the conflict between Sin and Grace, between this age and the new creation, there are resources for a healthy theology of the body for adolescent girls.

Elizabeth is a seventeen year old who had just completed the eleventh grade when we met. She is white. She was the only girl with whom I spoke who shared openly about how she deals with her own sexual desires. Britt Nicole alluded to it, saying she thinks girls are tempted just like boys are (although she went on to say boys are actually tempted more) by sexual activity. Elizabeth openly shared about how she finds sexual desire to be one of the most difficult things to deal with in terms of her theology of sin and temptation. She shared that the only way she knows how to not act on these desires is through masturbation, which she finds quite shameful. Girls are taught in school is that sexual desire is dangerous because of potential health risks and the possibility of pregnancy. The theology they are taught in churches is that sexual desire is prohibited and that their bodies cause this desire in others; thereby making their bodies particularly dangerous for the church. All the while, they are objectified in our society by the marketing of particularly young and female bodies, conveying that girls' bodies are a commodity to be traded in order to gain status and acceptance. Because teenage girls, like all adolescents, are experiencing their bodies and sexual desires in a new way, and because moralisms cut short their critical thinking skills and do not encapsulate the complexities they experience, a theology that is body-positive and desire-positive would be extremely helpful. Likewise, this kind of theology resists the dualism of body and soul.

Paul's new mortal body provides a biblical context and basis for this theology. The new mortal body is free from the power of Sin, and capable of operating in a new way, as part of the new creation now. Freedom from Sin is at the same time, freedom for living in partnership with God and in community with others. In Paul's worldview, the present time is a warzone between Sin and Grace, between Death and Life. For adolescent girls, their bodies become a battlefield in this cosmic conflict.

According to Paul, the believer has a new mortal body. This body is just as real, tangible, and fleshly as any body; it is not a spiritualized disembodied existence. The difference is that this new mortal body is not subject to Sin, though Sin will still try to exert its power and deceive the believer into being on its side in the ongoing conflict with Grace. Part of a corporate body of believers, each believer's body is free from the power of Sin: free to operate on the side of and with Christ. Each free body-in-community/body-in-Christ can work to liberate others. In other words, believers can participate with Christ and others who are in Christ in the liberation of other bodies. If a body is confined under Sin, it cannot help to liberate others. Ironically, girls' bodies are kept under Sin by (probably well-meaning) adults in their families, schools, and churches by teaching them to see their bodies as problematic and sources of temptation.

The fact that many of the girls I spoke with acknowledged their resistance to the body-shaming they received through their faith formation and participation in church is a sign of hope. Joyce Mercer writes that girls often participate in their own oppression by "de-selfing" themselves. [2] She observed in her interviews with adolescent girls that some of them "willingly diminished themselves in order to fit their own notions of gender difference." [3] Some of the girls, notably in the conversation with Britt Nicole and Genevieve, they were clearly "participating in their own oppression" [4] by accepting uncritically that they were at fault for making it difficult for boys to be good Christians. Britt Nicole felt that boys had it "almost" harder

---

2. Mercer, *Girltalk/Godtalk*, 61.

3. Mercer observes that girls participate in their own oppression by taking on society's expectations for what it means to be a girl or be feminine. She writes about their internalizing standards that ask them to be less than boys/men and to support gender inequality. She writes, "[i]f men were strong, women could be, too, only less so. If men were intelligent, so were women, but—at least at the level of appearances—they could not seem to be smarter than men, not if they wanted to be considered feminine." I observed girls participating in their own oppression, as well, though not as much when I asked them about the differences between boys and girl. Instead, I found this to be the case when they talked about their bodies, sin, and temptation. Their diminishing the power and goodness of their bodies to avoid being a threat to the Christian character or behavior of men fits into this same scheme. Girls felt the need to hide themselves and make less of themselves because to be their full embodied selves was too dangerous to boys/men. Ibid., 59.

4. Ibid., 60.

than girls when it came to avoiding sin and temptation. Genevieve said she understood that dressing so that a sports bra was showing was "too much" for boys to handle. She knew that she wanted to attract a good Christian boy to be her boyfriend, or eventual spouse, and that this was not possible if she did not cover her body "appropriately." Sam was caught between accepting what society says about the way girls dress and wanting an alternative. She notes that it's hard to not judge girls based on what they wear because she has been taught by society to think of girls who show their bra or wear short shorts and shirts as "sluts." On the other hand, she says that girls should be able to wear what they want to without being harassed.[5]

Censoring themselves in order to attract the "right" kind of guy or accepting uncritically that their bodies are problematic to boys seeking to be good Christians accepts the Christian cultural myth that the female body is sinful and causes others to sin. Sam is aware that she is accepting what society teaches about girls' dress revealing something about their sexual activity, that they are sluts. However, she is at a loss to know what else girls' dress might convey. She says that in her experience even if girls should be able to wear what they want without judgment, it seems like girls who chose "skimpy" clothes do so because they "want attention" or want to "show off something." Diminishing the goodness of their bodies and limiting the power of their bodies results in an "abdication of [their] personhood;"[6] humans are not human without their bodies. Nor are these girls who they are without their bodies.

The human body is not separate from the journey of faith. The body is not something to overcome in order for the soul to be saved. These girls have been taught that their bodies are the source of sinning for others; protecting the vulnerability and threat of their own bodies is how they can most please God with their bodies. They have not been taught or shown that their bodies are capable of righteousness or that their bodies are powerful in a positive way, that their bodies are how they show up in the world, or that their bodies are the source of their worship of God. For Paul, participation in Christ's death and resurrection happens with and in one's body, not separate from it.

The fact is that the human life is an embodied life. Pretending otherwise, or worse, shaming the body as a hindrance to abundant life for either the adolescent girl or others who observe or interact with her,

5. My term, not Sam's.
6. Mercer, *Girltalk/Godtalk*, 61.

perpetuates dualism and turns the adolescent girl's body over to Sin. This allows Sin to dictate the terms of acceptance of the body. It strips girls of the opportunity to use and love their bodies as sources of strength, power, and connection to the Holy. Church takes Sin's word for it that the body is necessarily dangerous, tempting, sinful, and something to be feared. In this contested liminal time, Paul says believers can dedicate their members (their bodies or members of their bodies or members of the corporate—*ecclesia*—body) to Sin or to God. Therefore, the task of liberative ministry with adolescent girls is about helping them dedicate their bodies to God's service, not by denying the body but by helping a person to use their embodied self for liberation.

Theology of the body guided by Pauline theology is challenging in practice in the context of the lives of adolescent girls. The reality is that while girls may feel they are exercising the power of their bodies by wearing revealing clothing, they may not be doing so as bodies free in Christ but instead as bodies being manipulated by Sin. It is true that the fashion industry is controlling what clothing is available to girls and is invested in objectifying and selling young women's bodies. In addition, girls should not be afraid of their bodies or ashamed of their sexual desires. It is also not the case that therefore they should engage in sexual activities that are unsafe to their developing bodies or psyches. That would certainly not be consistent with Paul's theology, which is that freedom in Christ leads to life.

SIN IS CONDEMNED

Given the girls' dissatisfaction with their own understanding of sin and their challenge with how relative it seems, Paul's concept of Sin can provide what they lack—a faithful understanding of sin apart of rules and regulations. For Paul, Sin is a power, an actor, a subject. People participate in Sin's action in the world when they sin.

At the heart of the question about Sin/sin is the question of how Paul views the human as a subject/agent. Most theologies of sin like those expressed by the girls in my interviews, maintain an anthropology in which the human subject is at the center. The human, imbued with a moral compass and perhaps guided by the Holy Spirit, chooses whether or not to commit a sin, whether or not to do an action which is sinful. Tay expresses this when she says that sin is "something that you do against God's will and that it's something that will add up to, like if you sin so much, you're gonna go to Hell." Britt Nicole's theology of sin is similar: "deviating from God's desires for us as his children." She also mentions that sin is unavoidable and part of being human. Sam said sin is "not doing the right thing . . . deviating from morals." The anthropology necessary for these theologies of sin is that the human is a free agent, able to make decisions either for good or for ill. In this theological anthropology, a person can then be held responsible for making those decisions, generally receiving justified punishment from God for deciding to sin and gaining appropriate acceptance from God for deciding not to sin. This idea is usually referred to as "free will." The human does things that are not in line with what God wants for him or her, and that is a sin. None of the girls mentioned that sin is something "left undone," a phrase that appears in two of the four prayers of confession in the United Methodist hymnal, for example.[7] The girls also did not mention that sinful action can happen without intention. They seem to assume that sinful action on their part is unavoidable and a problem with their wills, motives, and intentions.

Their theological anthropologies include a high view of human agency. The human is a free agent who can choose whether to sin or not. Their view of the human agent is in line with societal values in this country that laud autonomy. In addition, it gives the girls a feeling of strength and power in their own lives. If a girl can choose whether or not to sin, then she is powerful—able even to defy the will of God. Likewise, she is able to put her own will in line with God's. The power that a girl receives from this theology, however, is outweighed by the more problematic aspects of it. This model of agency is described by John Barclay as "competitive agency."[8] In this model, "the greater the affirmation of God's power (in strength or scope), the more inconsequential must be human agency . . . Whatever is attributed to free human agency must block or reduce divine agency."[9] In what most of the girls related about sin, their agency is great, and God is not able to stop them from sinning. They cannot stop themselves from sinning, either, so their agency is either limited in this way or their person is ultimately sinful, which would explain why they cannot stop themselves from sinning. They have a negatively deterministic view of human agency. God, their families, and their churches expect them to act in a way in which they are incapable of acting. God is demanding and places unrealistic expectations on them.

7. *The United Methodist Hymnal*, numbers 890 and 891.

8. Barclay, "Introduction," 6.

9. Ibid.

As Britt Nicole said, "[I]t's an inescapable as human beings in general." Certainly in this theology, God is needed to forgive humans for being human. God's grace becomes something humans need because they cannot measure up to the expectations that God creates for them. Or, in Tay's theology, there might even be a limit to the grace humans receive from God. If humans sin too much, they are rejected by God, period.

Much of what these girls shared about their lives is not about their own sinning, but about societal, systemic sin that plays out in their lives, though they did not call it out as such. Not one of the girls labeled sexism or racism a sin in our conversation around those topics. Raven talked about the false promise of the American dream, and Lena described her depression; Raven, Beverly, Dawn, and Monica talked about the violence against Black people in their community; Sam reflected on how she thinks her biological family would have wanted to keep her if she had been a boy; Genevieve talked about the pressure to keep boys from sinning by covering up her body; Tay shared the effects of the fashion industry on the self-esteem of her and her friends. Their limited understanding of sin as a human-willed action includes a rather negative image of God and of themselves. Additionally, their theologies of sin are unable to encompass and explain the systemic sin they experience.

Paul's theology explains that Sin is clearly at work in more complex ways than these girls have ability to articulate. He agrees that part of Sin involves human action; thus he tells the Roman Christians that they should not "present your members to Sin as instruments of wickedness" (Rom 6:13).[10] Importantly, however, human sinful action comes in the context of Sin as a subject/actor. Now that the Roman Christians are believers, they have the freedom not to submit to Sin's regime. This is true because the "sinful body" has been destroyed (Rom 6:6). They no longer belong to the sinful body as baptized believers, rather they belong to the body of Christ. Even with Tay's somewhat more nuanced view of sin when it comes to suicide, none of the girls conceived of Sin as an actor. This is a part of Paul's theology with which they have not interacted.

Paul's understanding of Sin as a power can provide girls with a theology of sin that includes not only human action, but also the systemic oppression of which they are objects. John Barclay explains another way divine and human agency operate in Paul in a model he calls

---

10. Capitalization of "Sin" is mine.

"non-contrastive transcendence," a concept he borrows from Kathryn Tanner. In this model of agency,

> God's sovereignty does not limit or reduce human freedom, but is precisely what grounds and enables it . . . But divine transcendence also here implies agencies that are non-identical: God is radically distinct from human agency and not an agent within the same order of being or in the same causal nexus. Thus human agency is neither an empty shell for divine power, nor a threat to divine agency—nor ultimately identical to divine agency. Rather, created human agencies are founded in, and constituted by, the divine creative agency, while remaining distinct from God.[11]

This model of agency comes closest to how I, and others, interpret Paul. The human agent is real and distinct from God, and is able to be free because of God. When the human agent is enslaved to Sin (Rom 6:20), it is not free. When the human agent is enslaved to righteousness, to God (Rom 6:22), it is free, and eternally so (Rom 6:23).

Adolescent girls are in an oppressed situation in this country. Not only are they undervalued because of their age, they are also the victims of sexism. Girls of color, girls who are in socio-economically depressed situations, girls who are immigrants, girls who do not fit beauty standards defined by the marketing industry, and girls who do not identify as cisgender and heterosexual are also victims of oppression for those reasons.[12] Paul's understanding of sin can speak directly into this reality and speak liberation to them. No longer is sin only something unavoidable that they do with their flawed or weak human agency acting out against the will of God, instead Sin is also something outside of themselves that they are not responsible for and from which they can be freed.

Girls who critically aware of systems of oppression, like Tay is of unrealistic beauty expectations perpetuated by the fashion industry, can have a theology that speaks into and about these forces. Now, however, instead of this being only something to deconstruct in an English term paper, girls can also have theological resources for understanding and deconstructing these forces. Girls who experience racist remarks on the subway, continue to see violence against members of their racial community, or are keenly

---

11. Barclay, "Introduction," 7.

12. "Cisgender" is a fairly recent term for the popular lexicon, though it is in most major dictionaries by now. It refers to a person whose gender identity corresponds to their sex at birth.

aware of privilege they enjoy because of their white skin color can now have theological resources to explain why this happens. There is a force outside of themselves, called Sin, which exerts pressure on human agents, even enslaves them in Paul's words. Being the victim of racism or sexism then is not strictly another human agent's fault, *nor is it their own fault*, rather this is how Sin is manifesting itself and holding human agents captive. Freedom from this captivity is exactly what happens through the faithfulness of Christ, something these girls can live into in the present even as they wait for the final conquering of Sin, which is still in the future.[13]

The truth is that becoming a Christian does not solve a girl's problems. Not only that, but girls see that Christians are not perfect people. Sin is still alive and well, even when girls are faithful members of their church and engaged in their own faith journeys. Sam stated that one of the biggest challenges to her faith is other Christians. She said that she noticed that Christians, "don't follow the ways of what, like, Jesus taught . . . Like being kind and stuff . . . I mean because of them, all Christians are hated on for being haters. Which is so weird . . . [I]f I just say [I'm a Christian], and I say it to a random person then . . . they're probably thinking that [I'm a hater]." Sam sees that being a Christian does not mean a person behaves the way Jesus would approve of. Moreover, Christians have a reputation for being haters.[14] Sam is concerned about what assumptions people might make about her when she tells someone she is a Christian. Presumably, those who do these kinds of things (act in a way contrary to Jesus' teaching or act like a hater) did these things before they became believers as well, as these are not marks of being in Christ.

Just as Sam can see the problems in behavior of some Christians, Raven can see problems in her own behavior and challenges in her faith journey. She recalls talking to a young adult in her congregation after an evening worship service about how she struggles even as a Christian:

---

13. The "faith[fulness] of Christ" is a lesser-known way to translate the genitive construction in some places, including Rom 3:21–22 and Gal 2:16. Another way to translate it is "faith in Christ," which puts the action in the anthropological realm instead of the Christological realm. Both ways of translating are grammatically correct based on the Greek. Simply given the high Christology in Paul's theology, the "faith[fulness] of Christ" seems a better translation choice. For a more comprehensive treatment of this, in regards to the Galatians verse specifically, see Richard Hays's book *The Faith of Jesus Christ*.

14. This is a popular slang term for a person who is jealous of or hates or disrespects others. There are varying nuances to how the term is used.

I was telling him, like, you know, "How can you be a Christian but still do all the stuff wrong that you do?" And I was talking to him about that cause I was having, like, a issue with my faith at the time. I think I was going through some stressful things. So, um, it kinda felt worse when I didn't feel that God was on my side. And um, like I won't lie, I don't exactly remember the words of the night that had me in tears, but, like, through that, through the man's sermon and then like [the young adult's] prayer it's almost like [the young adult] just answered my question . . . So he kinda, like, answered my question through his prayer and the guy had also mentioned it in the sermon so it's like my answers are being revealed and it's just like I started to have faith again. Like, maybe I'm not messing too far, maybe I didn't stray too far away from God because I was feeling like I'm not as bad as I thought. [I thought I was] on my way to Hell. Like, I really was far away from my need to be. And um, then, I don't know once they spoke and stuff I started to realize like, you know, I'm still on the right path. I may be turned a little bit but I can turn back around and stuff. So, I don't know, that was like the first like, okay, "this is God moment."

There are similarities between what Raven was relating as a particularly important moment in her faith journey and what Paul writes in Romans 7. Her question to herself, "How can you be a Christian but still do all the stuff wrong that you do?" echoes Paul's struggle with doing what he does not want to do. Like Paul, Raven's answer came through God's revelation in her life. Importantly for her, the answers came through worship (it was a youth-focused worship service with young adults and other adults working as mentors), through the prayer of a young adult and the sermon of another adult. This "God moment" for her was realizing that she was not beyond help, not on her way to Hell, not on the "wrong path." She had not strayed too far away from God. Paul's answer, too, is closeness with God. Nothing can separate him from the love of God in Christ (Rom 8:39). Not even Sin exercising its power in a believer's life and trying to wrest that believer from the Body of Christ and into its own service.

Paul's theological anthropology also raises important considerations about how other people influence a girl's sense of identity.[15] If there is no

15. Psychologist Jane Kroger explains identity formation this way, "an internal *developmental* transformation of the sense of self and consequent ways of filtering and making sense of one's life experiences. Intrapsychic restructuring during adolescence brings identity questions to the surface," *Identity in Adolescence*, 7. The adolescent girl needs to develop a sense of her "self." Moreover, the self they develop, their sense of "I" is not

free, autonomous individual, then whomever and whatever a girl associates with has a great deal to do with the person she is becoming and the person she perceives herself to be. If she is formed by people who understand her to be free from the power of Sin, then she, too, can see that she is free. If she is formed by people who understand her to be a sinner, unable to act without sin and without causing others to sin, then she, too, will see that she is connected with Sin above anything else. There are many de-formative experiences and influences that can negatively affect a girl's sense of self.

Many of the girls with whom I spoke seemed to suffer from low self-esteem. Different girls doubted their worth in different areas: physical beauty or size, intelligence, ability to achieve a goal for her life, or sense of general value as a person. A strong sense of self would help girls stand up for themselves, value themselves, and not accept the messages they receive from society or the church that are damaging to their wholeness. Churches who can value the selves girls bring to them and offer positive influences that encourage a strong sense of identity will be offering girls what they need to develop a sense of self that is in fact strong. Part of what Paul offers churches with his anthropology and theology of sin is help for a girl's developing sense of identity. Through Paul, the church can realize the importance of its role in not only helping a girl discover her own sense of self but also to realize that self is always a self-in-relationship, both with the church community and with the power of Grace under which it operates.

In Paul's theology expressed in Romans 6—8, it is not the case that the believer has naturally progressed to a better and more solid identity in Christ when he or she goes from not-being-in-Christ to being-in-Christ. The fact that Paul uses the passive voice to express that baptism happens to a person, shows that it is not human development or human progress that brings a person into Christ. It is assuredly the work of God. There is an abrupt change that happens in a person when they do become a believer. The metaphor of death that Paul uses expresses this quite clearly. However, someone who dies with Christ is not completely cut off from the person he or she was before, this is part of the challenge of living in the in-between time. This abrupt change is ultimately a change in epistemology, a change in the way they know their world, their community, their God, the anti-God powers, and themselves. They are now able to see reality as it is—a struggle between Sin and Grace where the final outcome of the battle has been decided, and it is that

---

predetermined. Social factors have a formative impact on this developing sense of "I."

Sin is defeated.[16] Martyn notes that God's "liberating invasion" is a revelation, an event that "brings about an epistemological crisis, a crisis in the way one sees and perceives."[17] Martyn calls this new perception "bifocal vision," which is to see "*both* the enslaving Old Age and God's invading and liberating new creation."[18] Importantly, for Paul, this new epistemology does not stop at vision, but also includes action. Now a believer knows they are free from the power of Sin and can live as subjects of their lives empowered by Grace and a part of a community in Christ. He or she can see how God is breaking in and can see the power of Sin for what it is. The believer is freed to act as God's instrument rather than Sin's. Once someone can see reality in this way, there is no going back. Even though one may still act in ways that support Sin in its mission, one will always see with this bifocal vision. Not only has God been revealed, so too has Sin been exposed.

Notably, Paul does not ask believers to repent of their sin.[19] Although they are free to operate under Grace now and not under Sin, they are not condemned for their difficulty in doing so (Rom 8:1). Nor is their absolution dependent on their asking for forgiveness, rather it is dependent on Christ's action. It does not show up in Romans 6–8. Instead, when Paul writes about Sin, he is writing about power. When he writes about humans, he writes about their freedom from the captivity to Sin and their freedom in Christ.[20]

The Christian community is an important part of being able to perceive the world for what it is and to see Sin for what it is. Turning to Martyn again, we see that Paul does something different than most Christians today expect when he tells Christians about what they are to do. Martyn writes that Paul does not contain any "decision-oriented ethics at all."[21] Given what the girls I interviewed shared concerning their beliefs about sin, this would be surprising for them to hear. Genevieve connects sin to decision-making:

16. Martyn, *Theological Issues*, 283.

17. Ibid., 284.

18. Ibid., 284, italics original.

19. Martyn notes that Paul hardly ever writes about repentance, ibid.

20. Interestingly, the United Methodist Eucharistic liturgies, *A Service of Word and Table* I and II, include Paul's apocalyptic worldview, though it is rarely, if ever, explained as such. It includes the statement of faith that Jesus "delivered us from slavery to sin and death." *United Methodist Hymnal*, 9, 13.

21. Martyn, *Theological Issues*, 233.

People try to forget that sin is a simple as telling a little lie or deceiving someone or wanting something that someone else. It can be so simple as that. I think people try to ignore that and it's really easy to. Because it's easier to push that away and be like, "I'm a Christian, I don't murder people so I'm not a sinner." It's hard to like remember that every day we sin 1000 times over but we can be forgiven for that, but it's tough to remember that sometimes and be like, "That's a sin. I need to not do that if I want to be a follower of God."

Tay sees sin as her action, and believes that if she sins too much she goes to hell. That Paul's expectations for believers' behavior is not about decision-making would come as good news to both of these girls. Humans are not called to act of their own free agency in ways that are either righteous or sinful. Instead, as persons in community (namely the community that is the Body of Christ), humans are shaped and empowered by the Spirit of Christ given to them to act as a community living the new life of Christ. Martyn writes that when Paul is speaking to the community it is *"newly addressable* because it bears Christ's form and is led by Christ's Spirit. That is to say, every one of Paul's hortatory sentences presupposes the presence of Christ and the constant activity of Christ's Spirit, as it causes the church to be able to hear."[22] The community is newly addressable because it is now free from Sin. As a free community participating in Christ's resurrection, assured of its own resurrection, and empowered by the Spirit, it is now able to respond from that freedom in its actions in the world. Paul does not address individual believers; he addresses the community as a whole, which has been freed from Sin. This is consistent with his anthropology.

In this anthropology and view of Sin, there is also new opportunity for girls to denounce the ways in which their own Christian communities have acted contrary to their liberation from Sin. Many of the girls I interviewed had grievances against their churches. Many could point to ways their churches had contributed to their feeling shameful about their bodies. When I asked Tay what has impacted her faith in a negative way, she shared with me that former pastors of her church had acted like gatekeepers telling her she was not really welcome in the church because her opinions differed from theirs. She credits the denominational youth organization that is separate from the local church with giving her a space where she actually wanted to claim that she was a Christian: "It was basically just after realizing that [my pastors can't control how I think], nothing else really deterred

---

22. Ibid., italics original.

me from feeling closer to God, it was just from then on it was all the pastors and the people in my church that were giving me a bad vibe about it, and I was just like, I have no problem with being Christian, I'm proud of being Christian. I feel like it kind of makes me stronger." In this instance, she felt that her church had made it harder to be a Christian, but this outside group helped her be stronger in her faith and stay close to God despite her experience in her local church.

When Monica shared that racism was discussed in her church but that sexism was "taboo," she pointed to another way the church has not been the community adolescent girls need. Not only has the church perpetuated cultural myths that teenagers have nothing to share and that their young, female bodies are responsible for the sins of others, but the teenagers have also heard silence on topics that matter a great deal to them. Their experiences have largely not been welcomed into their churches and their struggles are not being addressed. Churches are failing to offer girls a theological lens with which to interpret their lives in life-giving ways. The theological lens many churches do offer is one that echoes society's values and judgments about girls. In taking seriously Paul's concept of Sin, the girls can call out the church for these practices as being part of Sin's action in the world rather than action that is consistent with its identity as the Body of Christ.

HOPE

In addition to Paul's theology around body and sin, there are several other smaller but related topics in Paul's theology that are important for liberative ministry with adolescent girls. Hope is one of them. Romans 8:24–25 says, "For in hope we were saved. Now hope that is seen is not hope. For who hopes for what is seen? But if we hope for what we do not see, we wait for it with patience." When I asked the girls I interviewed what they hope for, I was struck by how little their hopes rested on some change for them in the present.

They hoped for a good Christian spouse in the future. Grace, a girl whom I interviewed who suffered from selective mutism and whose friend became her mouthpiece when she could not speak to others, hoped that when she went to college away from her friend, they would still be able to maintain their friendship.[23] Dawn, Monica, and Raven all expressed not wanting to struggle so much financially, wanting to be able to pay their

---

23. For more information on these two girls and their interview, see the Appendix.

bills without worry. Raven and Dawn want work that is fulfilling. Raven expresses her desire to be a lawyer in terms that sound vocational, something she always wanted deep down inside. Monica does not want to worry about illness. Raven also uses theological language about what she hopes for, that she is hoping for "doing everything that God set for you."

In talking to these girls, I did not get the feeling that their hopes for happiness were the kind of hopes critiqued as being part of Moralistic Therapeutic Deism (MTD).[24] They were not talking about shallow or merely self-serving happiness. For the girls whose families struggled financially, their hopes were to not have those struggles for themselves in their future. Their hopes for the future reflected the difficulties of their present situation. Hoping for vocational fulfillment in work also did not seem to be a shallow desire; rather it again was a response to present difficulties.

Sadie expressed a different hope than did other girls I interviewed. Her hopes reflect her social situation as well. As a white person who attends school with many racial minorities, is questioning her sexuality, and has dealt with explicit sexism and unwanted advances of at least one male, she has had a unique set of experiences both of privilege and of oppression. Her hopes for her future include an explicit desire to help others. She said, "I wanna dream really big . . . there's so many things that I see that should be like, fixed. And I don't really wanna fix them I just wanna . . . do something impressive . . . I don't really know what I wanna do specifically. I wanted be an ice cream truck driver when I was little. I feel like that [would bring happiness]. Or like, be the president; that would be cool, too." Sadie's church is extremely socially active, with social issues at the forefront of their worship and outreach life. Her hopes express her formation in that community—she is aware that there are a lot of problems and wants to be a part of fixing them. She did not share what would make her happy; she shared that she wants to help others be happy, though her method to doing so (ice cream truck driver) would not fix the systemic problems that cause unhappiness.

Sam, who is also a part of Sadie's congregation, at first seemed to voice a dream that did sound like MTD. When asked what her biggest hopes were, Sam responded that she wanted to go to the Tony's or the Oscar's. As

24. Moralistic Therapeutic Deism (MTD) is a term coined in the groundbreaking book *Soul Searching* in 2005. After extensive interviews with youth all over the country, Christian Smith and Melinda Denton determined that whether religious or not, the faith of the American teenager can be called MTD. Some of the hallmarks of this faith is that God wants people to be happy and that good people go to Heaven when they die. *Soul Searching*, 162–63.

our conversation continued, however, it became clear that this was not a dream about being around celebrities or about being famous herself; this was instead about her vocation. As someone gifted in behind-the cameras work like set design, she began to talk about how girls need to know that there are options available to them that our gendered society does not show as possibilities for them, specifically more "manual labor" options. She noted that this kind of work is not seen as "girly" and that women who, for example, work in construction, are seen as "worthless." Going to the Tony's or Oscar's is her dream to show other girls that this kind of work is for girls, too. I asked Sam how or if she thought her church has been a part of helping her to know what kind of options are available for her outside of the traditional ones girls are often taught. She talked about how she wants to be involved in theater or film. There are people in her congregation who are involved in those fields, which shows her that those are viable career options for her. She said that the church should be able to help girls discover these alternative options because, "it's partly their job to like raise you, sort of. Um, to help you. To help anyone, I guess, is their job." For Sam, her hope of being involved in the Tony's or Oscar's is her hope of having worked on a film or theater project that reaches the top recognition in the country. The way she found that this is her vocation is through her hands-on involvement in various ministries of the church that include theater, but also marches, helping the homeless, community service, and gardening. She sees that the church has been a vital part of helping to raise her and show her different ways in which she can be active that other places in her life (she specifically mentioned her school) do not.

Evelyn Parker writes about the difference between emancipatory hope and wishful thinking in her book, *Trouble Don't Last Always: Emancipatory Hope Among African American Adolescents*. She defines wishful thinking as "a desire and a longing void of possibility and personal agency."[25] It is fantasy, something that will not come true. Hope is different. Hope is "associated with expectancy, confidence, assurance, and faith."[26] Parker sees that emancipatory hope is an alternative to wishful thinking and a powerful "theological framework for congregations that are intentional about fostering hope in African American teenagers through ministry with them."[27] Emancipatory hope looks for transformation of social systems that are un-

25. Ibid.
26. Ibid.
27. Ibid.

just. It means "freedom from domination" and is "to expect that hegemonic relations will be transformed and to acknowledge personal agency in God's vision for human equality."[28] Not only does this theological framework speak into the experience and needs of many of the girls I interviewed, this concept of emancipatory hope is also consistent with Paul's theology of hope, sin, human agency, and new creation.

Of the girls whose voices feature prominently in this book, Raven, Dawn, and Monica are Black. They expressed their hopes in terms of what will make them happy in the future. Their hopes for meaningful work and economic security reflect their experiences based largely on their position in society as Black girls. Although these girls all expressed awareness of and frustration with the racism of our society, which they have experienced throughout their lives, the hopes that they shared with me were not hopes for dismantling racism. Emancipatory hope, as Parker envisions it being fostered in African American congregations, would help them confront systems that limit and form their experiences and their hopes with powerful expectation and action for dismantling them.

Paul's worldview as expressed in Romans 6–8 offers biblical grounding for just this kind of expectant hope. Paul writes about hope explicitly in ch. 8, though it is also implicit in chs. 6 and 7. Explicitly, Paul writes that hope is for that which is not yet realized, something that cannot be seen, and that hope is a soteriological recognition of Christ's action ("in this hope we were saved" 8:24). He also says that we wait with patience for our hope to be seen (8:25). This hope is for the new creation for which creation waits, groaning for it with labor pains. Therefore this is not futile patience or wishful thinking; it is deep hope for that which is coming, that which is already in the process of being birthed. This is how believers know that this hope is not wishful thinking; it is already in the process of being fulfilled, though its birth is still in process. The childbirth pains are not yet done.

In this largely instructive section of Romans (chapters 6–8), Paul's use of the imperatives show that Paul expects that believers can live into the vision of the new creation even though present creation still waits for its arrival. This is the hopeful expectation of Paul for the Roman community and for adolescent girls in this century. Being in Christ means believers have the ability and the imperative to live in the present as if God's hope for creation is realized. The ability to do so comes because, although believers are not

28. Ibid, 15.

yet resurrected, through their baptism they can participate with Christ in his resurrection, which has assuredly already happened.

The hopes and dreams the girls I interviewed gave voice to were hopes and dreams about their future. As they grappled with the challenges of the present, the hopes they voiced were delayed. This was true for girls regardless of their race or class. Paul places hope in the present, and pairs it with patience and with action. Paul's theology is not that believers wait for the new creation with patience while waiting for God to act; rather it is that while in the present and waiting for the new creation, believers act as if the new creation is already here. Although the battle between Sin and Grace still rages, believers are firmly on the side of Grace. They are able to be instruments of that Grace now; there is no condemnation now; they are slaves to righteousness now; they are free from Sin now.

For adolescent girls today, there are important implications for the believers' call to live in the present as if the new creation is already here. Girls can realize that the power of Sin is outside of themselves, thus sin is neither only immoral action on their part that deviates from God's will nor something inherent to their female bodies. Girls have the power of Christ, as part of the body of believers who are in Christ, to confront the systemic Sin that tries to enslave them and to know without a doubt that this Sin is ultimately defeated. Paul's theology gives them power to partner with Christ in defeating the racism, classism, sexism, and heterosexism that is constantly telling these girls lies about themselves. They are no longer objects of oppression, but subjects in Christ in defeating the very powers that try to subject them to dehumanization. These girls can live as fully free human subjects now, as they wait with patience and promise for Sin to be finally and fully defeated.

WHAT THEN SHOULD WE DO?

Paul's expectation is not for believers to make the right ethical decisions and thus live a righteous life. His expectation is for them to live a free life enslaved to righteousness that will show God as they live. The terminology of enslavement is challenging for several reasons. The history of the United States offers devastating proof of the lack of righteousness when we consider the slavery of Africans and African Americans for generations and the ongoing effects of slavery in a society that is founded on inequality and abuse of other humans. When Raven was considering racism and this country's history of slavery, she said, "I don't know, like, when you just look back in history and you see how things weren't even, you just see how things are going now it's kind of like, it's still here." Although there is no longer state-sanctioned or legal slavery now, Raven notes that things are not that much different. She was specifically reflecting on violence against the Black community in her city. Not only do we have historical and current reason to bristle at the term and reject it, but also to think of enslavement, even to God, as a positive goes against our culture's aspiration for an individual's autonomy and freedom.

Given Paul's anthropology, however, there is no way for a human to exist without falling under some power or lordship, as Käsemann wrote. Because Christ has invaded this realm, humans can now be free from the power of Sin and instead operate under the power of Grace, humans have been released from their slavery to Sin and can now be enslaved to righteousness. Freedom from Sin is freedom to be in Christ and live accordingly.[29] To live in this way, however, is not based on a person making a decision to do so. Enslavement to God comes through baptism and participation in Christ's resurrected life in community. Righteous action on the part of humans is action on the side of Grace against Sin. This is exactly the kind of action girls are both looking for from their churches and are capable of themselves when they are in Christ.

Paul's worldview was not limited to understanding, intellectual assent or simply "a perspective." Included in his worldview is the necessity of action, both as a response to the realities of it and as part of how it is constructed. Through his engagement with real life issues effecting the communities to which he wrote, he found evidence of the powers of both Sin and Grace. Through his experience of Jesus Christ in his own life, he saw the world completely differently and acted completely differently as a result. His letters were written to enable people to see differently and live differently. He believed that seeing the world as it really is happens through experience and because of it; he trusted that his letters would be just such an experience.

Some of the girls I interviewed talked about the importance of Christian friendship. Kaia is a 17-year-old Caucasian who just finished her junior year. She shared with me the importance of her friendship with the girls in her church. In our interview, she shared that her friends who are

---

29. Käsemann writes about the necessity of action on behalf of God, which he alternatively calls "service to God" and "bodily obedience" (*Romans*, 177).

not in her youth group are a source of temptation for her but that her youth group friends are a source of strength. She said, "Because people really do some horrible things. But luckily we have each other and I don't think, like, any of us do, like, bad things, like, we all hang out with each other on Friday nights instead of partying and everything." Genevieve shared that while she was away at a "pre-college summer course thing," she found herself thinking differently than when she was with her youth group friends and voiced surprise at how she saw herself changing in different company. She made friends in the summer program who were talking about their sexual experiences and about having bought a pregnancy test for a friend. From hanging around these girls, she began to feel like she should have experiences like this. When reflecting on that she said, "And I was, like, 'I'm embarrassed. I'm not going to tell them that I've never had a first kiss because that's so embarrassing.' But I had to take a step back and go, 'Wait, I'm proud of this. I have friends who are also doing this and I'm not alone in this and it's okay.'" Genevieve had to remember herself and her group of Christian friends while she was away from them in order to remember her values and her worth as defined by God instead of by the number of boys she had (or had not) hooked up with. She made it clear that it is because of her Christian values that she does not hook up with guys, and that she though these girls in her pre-college program were getting their self-worth from their physical relationships with boys. As girls confront the power of Sin, their Christian friendships provide a safe place from which to gain freedom from that power.

Sadie is an example of a girl who has gifts for the church and is at a church that welcomes those gifts. At age 15, Sadie is aware of her white privilege, critical of it, and conflicted by how to understand her white privilege while still suffering from sexism and heterosexism. She gets some of the highest grades in her school. She looks with wonder at the world around her, and appreciates learning new things about her surroundings. She is strong and outspoken, while also being sensitive and careful. She values strength in others and appreciates those who are just comfortable being their unique selves. Her church has been a powerful and positive part of her life and has shaped her own faith greatly. She says that her church "is good because it, um, it sends the message of love. Almost overpoweringly, and sometimes a little bit *oof*, but like there' like the message of acceptance and love and sort of action, and, oh, like that we are in this world to change this world, and as Christians were should do what Jesus taught, which is love and forgiveness, and helping." She is able to identify her own gifts, which she has come to learn about through her involvement at church.

Interestingly, she contrasts her church to other churches she has heard about from her friends saying, "I have friends who, um, go to different types of churches where all they do is, like, go to church. And like talk about, talk about sins and stuff." Sadie has not been taught, or has at least not absorbed, a theology of sin like Paul's that would connect many of the injustices of which she is aware. She sees that focusing on "sins and stuff" is the opposite of her church's teachings about acceptance, love, forgiveness, and action. Paul's worldview, including his understanding of Sin and the Christian community's freedom to join in the fight against Sin would offer her a powerful theological lens through which to see the importance of the action of her church and how her self-identified gift from God can be used in this fight.

Tay is an example of a teenager whose church does not welcome her gifts. In fact, she has been able to embrace her gifts in spite of her church and the pastors she has experienced in church leadership.[30] Tay is bright and passionate about her love for music and photography. She is in touch with her emotions and a fiercely loyal friend. She cares deeply about people and about the church; though she is not shy of being critical of both, offering truths that need to be taken seriously if our churches are to fulfill their calling to be a community that welcomes all members of the Body of Christ. She is quick to notice hypocrisy, in herself and others. She is self-aware. She expects more of the church than it offers. Although she has found Christian community through the denominational ministry of which she is a part, she is still disappointed by her local church and wants them to be more accepting and loving of her and the ways God speaks in her life. She is one of the young women with whom I spoke who is aware of societal pressures, especially as it relates to female body size and clothing, but has not heard these issues discussed or criticized in church. Paul's theology about Sin would be of great use to Tay to offer her a way to theologically explain these pressures, as well as other issues that are close to her heart like self-injury and suicide. In fact, much of what she experiences is decidedly not welcome in the church, as she has received harsh pushback when bringing up these experiences in the church. Tay is looking for action from her church on matters of great importance to her, but it is

---

30. Tay's current pastor is a welcome change. She finds him approachable and welcoming of her, though her church community at large is unchanged.

missing. Paul's theology of eschatological reservation may help her understand the limitations of her church community and remain connected with them as they struggle to remain the church in these times. However, in the absence of engaging seriously with this kind of theology, Tay is left seeing her church as impotent around what matters most to her and inviting her in only on the condition that she leave her criticisms, her gifts, her experiences, her body, in short herself, outside.

VIOLENCE

The fact that Paul uses language of conflict and violence is at least as disturbing as his use of slave language. Paul does not see that the present time is a neutral time where someone can choose whether or not to operate under Sin or under Grace. His language clearly reflects that it is not a person's individual decision about which power they fall under, and also that the present time is one of violent conflict between the two powers of Sin and Grace. Death is on both sides of the battle. Sin's partner is Death; but when one falls under Grace, one has already died (in Christ). Death is also not neutral. Its power over humanity is broken by Christ, who offers eternal resurrected life. Life is on the side of Christ, Death is on the side of Sin. Humans are also not neutral. As one is freed from Sin by Christ, they can either present their members to Sin's forces against Grace or they can present their members to Grace's forces against Sin.

For girls who endure violence in their own lives and whose communities suffer violence, Paul's words about the present time being one of violent conflict ring true. It is important that in reading Paul's account of reality we are aware that he is not suggesting that believers create violent situations or interact with their world violently. In telling the Roman Christians about the world around them and the cosmic conflict in which they play a part, Paul is not prescriptive, rather he is descriptive. The truth is that Sin is a powerful, violent force. Sin seeks death and makes use of what should have been life to cause death. Sin is against life. Paul's understanding of the implication of Christ's invasion into this world makes sense with the experience of adolescent girls.

The clash between Sin and Grace can offer a theological lens for girls to understand and interpret their experiences of violence. All that works for death is on the side of Sin. Being enlisted in Sin's army means being paid in death. The Black girls I spoke with who shared with me about racial violence in their community and around the country know what Death looks like. It looks like unarmed Black teenagers being killed by white men. It looks like a man shot in his own home by police who were not punished. It looks like death down the block from their church. It looks like excessive violence. Raven related the stories of the death of Black men in her community listing off several cases, ending with the question about why it seems inappropriate to point out that those who are killing Black men are white.

Sadie also told me about an experience of violence. A boy who was a part of one of the outreach ministries of the church and had started coming to the youth group had run away from home. Sadie and her mom found him on the subway and brought him back to their house. They had gone up to her room to use the computer and she said he was not acting like himself, he was talking fast and "crazy." He tried to physically force her to kiss him, and she was terrified of what else he might try. She got out of the situation and went to her parents for support. He ended up leaving their home. After that, Sadie shared that "like every single person who looked anything like him, like I would like [get scared], like on the subway . . . that's also made me really scared. Of getting attacked."

Girls experience the violence of the world; these two examples of what Raven and Sadie shared do not exhaust their exposure to violence. Paul's understanding that this present time is a time of conflict is descriptive not only of what is happening in the cosmos between forces of Sin and Grace, but also in the lives of these adolescent girls. Violence is a fact of life for these girls, a fact Paul understands quite well.

In the present time, as Paul writes in ch. 6, believers are to yield the members of their corporate body to God. This is where his prescription for dealing with the violence he has so aptly described comes in. In the conflict, which is as large as the cosmos and as personal as the very bodies of believers, there are no innocent bystanders. According to Paul's anthropology, humans are either on the side of Sin or on the side of Christ. Paul's charge is not for believers to combat violence with violence, but to be aware of the violent battle raging around them and through them, and to recognize their freedom to be alive in the face of death. Paul tells the hearers of his letter to be on the side of Christ, the side of life. Life is the opposite of death, the opposite of the violence these girls experience that diminishes or ends life.

chapter 4

CONFRONTING THE POWERS
IN COMMUNITY

"Let me paint a picture for you then I'll have to teach you to see it"

—Sara Bareilles[1]

Sara Bareilles's song, *Eden,* powerfully describes for me a guide for educating adolescent girls in the church, especially as informed by Paul's letters. We need to paint the picture of our lives, and we need to teach others how to see those pictures. This educational endeavor includes reciprocal teaching, reorientation of perspective, and responsive action. Girls need to paint the pictures of their lives and teach adults how to see their pictures the way they themselves do so that the adults can both understand girls' lives and be allies with them.

Adults cannot understand what is going on for girls without this instruction. Adults must be willing to learn from girls. Girls must be willing to teach. Adults and girls both need to share their stories with each other. The texts of our lives are a large part of the content of this pedagogy, as is true for other liberative pedagogies. The kind of challenges that girls face are similar to the ones that adults have been facing since their own adolescence even as there will be some differences. The kind of community that can be formed through sharing stories adults to youth is powerful in both its vulnerability and its strength. At the same time adults and youth need to teach each other how to see their own paintings differently. A Pauline lens might be a new one for everyone. The world is different than we have been led to believe and it will be a challenge to put on these new

1. Sara Bareilles, "Eden" on *The Blessed Unrest,* compact disc.

lenses, keep these lenses on, and act in a response-able way from seeing differently through them.

Christian education can be defined as the "processes by which people learn to become Christian and to be more Christian, through their learning Christian beliefs, attitudes, values, emotions and dispositions to engage with Christian actions and to be open to Christian experiences."[2] Or as Thomas Groome puts it, Christian education is about teaching the "Christian faith as a way of the head, a way of the heart, and a way of the hands."[3] Christian education is about helping Christians be more fully Christians in who they are, what they know, and their actions in the church and world. The Pauline pedagogy, this way of educating into the new creation, that I am presenting here is exactly this: a way for girls and women to be more Christian in their being, knowing, and doing, and lead others in doing the same. This is a way for adolescent girls and the adults who minister with them to grow in practicing their faith in their daily lives and as they reflect on their experiences in community.

Paul's letters show that seeing the world for what it is is a profoundly theological and counter-cultural way to interpret life; and that life changes as a result. Paul is a resource for helping girls learn how to live a Christian life; it comes through seeing the world as Paul did. They can only do so if they are involved in intentional interpretation of their life stories and involved in helping others in their own interpretative work. This pedagogy is necessarily communal, transformative, and both inspires and requires action toward justice in the world.

Paul's own "paintings," which we have as his epistles, offer a new, different, and liberating perspective on the world, as I have already shown. These letters show girls why the struggles they face are so real. They can help release girls from bondage to the idea that sin is only about bad decisions they make or an inherent part of their makeup as a female human. They can contextualize suffering and offer hope to one another. Both adults and girls need a perspective shift, they need to see differently. The educational model I am proposing is a journey of discovery for girls and for the adults who minister with them. This indeed is a process for these girls and women to become more Christian. They learn to see their own lives,

2. Jeff Astley and Colin Crowder, "Overview" in *Theological Perspectives on Christian Formation*, edited by Jeff Astley, Leslie J. Francis, and Colin Crowder, x.

3. Thomas Groome, *Will There Be Faith?*, 111. Groome writes about the hands as being about action, the heart as being about right relationships and desires and attitudes, and the head being about "faith seeking understanding."

the lives of those around them, and in fact the whole of creation with eyes changed by the Christian Scriptures. They learn the Christian practices of deeply listen to one another and choosing action based on their discoveries about each other and the world in which they live.

This book is a contribution to Christian religious education, and to youth ministry as a part of that larger field. I rely on the dynamic and passionate work of Christian educators and scholars of youth ministry. This is also a practical theology of youth ministry with girls that is empowered by Paul; this is what I call "educating into the new creation." In this chapter, I will offer some examples of the work of Christian educators and scholars of youth ministry that provide the setting into which this book fits. I will then offer my own methodology—a proposal for a new way to do youth ministry in the church. The examples at the end of this chapter show just how powerful this new way to do youth ministry is for adolescent girls, the adults who are in ministry with them, their churches, and their wider communities.

THE LANDSCAPE OF CHRISTIAN RELIGIOUS EDUCATION

Educating into the new creation is part of the continually developing landscape of Christian education, which helps inform, transform, and form Christians into people of deeper and more vibrant faith. For decades the field of youth ministry has been making the case that adolescents are an essential part of the church and should not be kept separate from other faithful members of their churches. This idea first gained traction with Kenda Creasy Dean and Ron Foster's book, *The Godbearing Life*. In that book, published in 1998, Dean and Foster convincingly reject the typical youth ministry model where youth have worship, fellowship, and education separate from the rest of the church. Youth need, and want, to be a part of the church, connected with adults who can know them, love them, teach them, and model what adult Christian faith can look like and be like. Otherwise, they argued, youth graduate out of church when they graduate out of the youth group.[4] Many other scholars have followed their lead, writing about the importance of meaningful adult interaction with adolescents in the life and education of the church.[5] The expansive research conducted

---

4. Dean and Foster, *The Godbearing Life*, 30.

5. For example, DeVries, *Sustainable Youth Ministry*; Dean, *Almost Christian*; Myers, *Black and White Styles of Youth Ministry*.

by the National Study on Youth and Religion as presented in *Soul Searching* by Christian Smith with Melinda Lundquist Denton has left little room for those who think keeping youth separate from the church is an effective way to help nurture their faith as adolescents and prepare them for a life of Christian faith and practice as they grow up.

Part of what that research also showed is that the majority of teenagers in the United States are incredibly inarticulate about their faith. Smith and Denton point out that when young people are asked about their lives, they are quite articulate about all kind of different aspects of their lives, but not so about their faith.[6] Michael Warren wrote about the silence of youth in his *Youth, Gospel, Liberation*, which was published back in 1987. He said that youth have been silenced in their public life. He wrote, "It is only later as older adults that they are able to look back and speak of the earlier period, the period of silence, the period of systematic inarticulateness . . . [V]ery few young people are ever encouraged to take their life experience seriously enough to want to articulate it.[7] The voice Warren notes as missing is specifically a public voice, one he notes does show up in "the original depictions of their own lives which they write for the literary magazines published each year by most high schools and colleges."[8]

Scholars of Christian religious education have noticed for some time, therefore, that keeping youth separate from the rest of the church inhibits their faith development and forms them to be silent. Since the time of Warren's book and Smith and Denton's as well, the way that young people communicate has changed vastly. For example, Facebook began in 2004 as a social network for college students. In the more than ten years since then, however, many other parts of the population, including many teenagers, have joined that and other social networks through the internet. In October of 2014, Facebook released their quarterly report, which included that there are 1.35 billion monthly active users, about the same number as the population of China.[9] Although social networking can seem private, and certainly has well-documented drawbacks and dangers, through it young people do develop a public voice and public persona both as individuals

6. Smith and Denton, 131.

7. Warren, *Youth, Gospel, Liberation*, 14.

8. Ibid.

9. Caitlin Dewey, "Almost as many people use Facebook as live in the entire country of China," *The Washington Post*, October 29, 2014 and accessed January 6, 2015, http://www.washingtonpost.com/news/the-intersect/wp/2014/10/29/almost-as -many-people-use-facebook-as-live-in-the-entire-country-of-china/.

and as a group. Social media provides a new public space for youth to author these "original depictions of their life."

Perhaps the practice of social networking has aided young people in gaining a public voice and the ability to become more articulate. What I observed in my small sampling of girls in the New York Area was that they are articulate about their lives *and* their faith, when they are asked to do so and given space to answer. When they did not know what they believed, many of them wrestled with the question in conversation with me; in those instances, it was clear that they had not really thought about it before. In some of the group interviews, the girls questioned each other and pushed each other as they worked to articulate their beliefs and even tease our the implications those beliefs have for their lives. Youth cannot be expected to be articulate about something they have never had practice voicing. These interviews offered an opportunity to do just that.

Girls have not, for the most part, been encouraged to be articulate about themselves, and have not been given the theological tools to understand themselves either. Churches are hesitant to explore the complexities of being an adolescent girl, defaulting to moralisms (don't have sex before you're married, cover your body, don't tempt boys) or to ignoring these complexities all together. If silence is presumed a positive quality for all youth in general, it is even more so the expectation for girls, who are not only young but also female. Society (including the church) still devalues the female voice and does not concentrate on helping girls develop a strong voice so that they will be strong women. The recent campaign drawing attention to how girls are often called "bossy" when exhibiting leadership skills shows that this is an ongoing problem.[10] Moreover, some churches have failed to offer the radical counter-cultural approach to living that I have identified from Pauline theology.

If girls are to learn to articulate their faith, they need to be invited into the practice of speaking out loud. In her 1977 essay *Beloved Image*, Nelle Morton tells a story about a small group of women who had come together to listen and share their stories. In recounting how one woman in the group told her story, Morton describes the deep kind of listening that took place as, "A hearing engaged in by the whole body that evokes speech—a new

---

10. Sheryl Sandberg and Anna Maria Chávez, "Sheryl Sandberg and Anna Maria Chávez on 'Bossy,' the Other B-word," *Wall Street Journal*, updated March 8, 2014 and accessed January 15, 2015, http://www.wsj.com/articles/SB10001424052702304360704579419150649284412.

speech—a new creation. The woman *had* been heard to her own speech."[11] Hearing someone into speech is empowerment, and it is a new creation. What is created was not there before. A person speaks, a person is heard, a story is found and shared, change takes place.

Dori Baker, in *Doing Girlfriend Theology*, looks to Nelle Morton's "hearing to speech" as foundational to her own practice of girlfriend theology.[12] Girlfriend theology is a practice of opening a space in a small group community for girls to share meaningful stories from their lives and to seek to connect those stories to God's story through a process of group discernment so that new images of God that help create new relationships with God emerge. Like with Morton's example of a small group of women sharing stories, Baker finds that in a small group of women and girls sharing stories, both the speaker of the story and her hearers are transformed. She agrees with Morton that what is created in these instances of hearing to speech is something new, "Being called forth to speech is not a solitary act of personal devotion, but a political one; it names and new reality and creates a community with the potential to effect change."[13] Baker sees the possibility for change to occur with the new creation that emerges from the telling and listening process. For the girls I interviewed, this is one of the most important promises their churches can provide.

Like Baker, I found that hearing these girls to speech was a transformational practice. I opened a space through our conversations that did not exist before. They entrusted their stories to me, and both asked and answered new questions. In the group interviews, they challenged each other and pushed each other. In the one-on-ones they told me they had never had the opportunity to talk about this kind of thing before. One conversation where this freedom to speak was clearly happening for the first time was with a fourteen year old, who ended up spitting question after question out to me, almost faster than her mouth could keep up. After several minutes of these questions, she took a deep breath and asked why she couldn't do this at church all the time. Asking me questions about life and faith opened something new in her. I have no doubt that the interviews I conducted were acts of creation. I also see the limits of those conversations because I am not in an ongoing relationship with the girls. There are limits perhaps especially for the girls I

---

11. Nelle Morton, *The Journey is Home*, 128.

12. Baker, *Girlfriend Theology*, 30.

13. Ibid.

spoke with one-on-one because they were not with peers with whom they can continue the practice after our interviews ended.

Hearing the girls to speech is a beginning, and a very important one. It is also only a beginning. Sharing their stories and having them heard must lead to concrete action in response. Articulating faith is not the end goal, it is just one step toward living more Christian lives in the world. Action in response to the sharing and hearing their stories can be in small and personal ways, or in larger ways that can affect change in their churches or even society at large. For girls who are formed into silence by society and by the church, the act of hearing them to speech is a dramatic counter-cultural act of rebellion. Those who were silenced can speak and their words can be public, political, and can affect change. This, after all, is what happens with the words Paul shared through his letters, too.

Christian education insists that faith is not only knowledge about Christianity, God, the Trinity, etc. It is not only a set of beliefs one hold privately in one's heart or inward disposition. Christianity is also an *active faith* because belief compels action in the world on behalf of God, inspired by the Spirit, and toward the continued building of the kin-dom of God on earth. Teaching youth to think theologically and interpret their lives theologically means that they will act in their churches, schools, and the world as faithful Christians building the kin-dom of God.

Scholars have been pushing youth ministries to be more theologically rich in recent years. Andrew Root in *Revisiting Relational Youth Ministry* made a case for youth workers to understand their own role more theologically. Root argues that in relationships between youth and between youth and their youthworkers, the object is to love the other person and in so doing Christ is incarnated.[14] The goal, then, of youth ministry is no longer to get kids in the church or teach kids not to have sex; instead the goal of youth ministry is to love youth. Concretely loving youth through youth ministry is also to offer them space to explore the rich theology of the Christian faith. Young people need to ask questions, doubt, wonder, celebrate, and create and do all of this in an environment that is teaching them to interpret it all theologically.[15] As young people learn to interpret life theologically and articulate their own faith as it is growing, changing,

---

14. Andrew Root, *Revisiting Relational Youth Ministry*, especially chapter 5.

15. Andrew Root and Kenda Creasy Dean argue for this necessity, and offer many different examples of teaching youth to think theologically in their book *The Theological Turn in Youth Ministry*.

and developing, they become more mature in faith and their actions will be more reflective and more faithful.

Thomas Groome's *Sharing Faith* insists that Christian education is about doing God's will in the living out of the Christian faith as much as it is about knowing about Christianity and believing in it.[16] Evelyn Parker in *Trouble Don't Last Always*, referenced in chapter 3, constructs a method of Christian education that shapes emancipatory hope in ministry with African American teenagers. This kind of hope is "illustrated by movements that seek freedom from domination."[17] It is not enough that girls share their stories in small groups with other girls and women. Girls need to bring their lives into the sanctuary and sent through the doors of the sanctuary and into the world. Educating into the new creation is ultimately education for the entire Body of Christ. Moreover, not just any action will do. Their action must be toward the liberation of those who held captive by Sin and living in an old world even though the new creation has broken in.

Given Paul's understanding of the present time being one of conflict in which Sin seeks to take over people's agency, girls need peer and adult companions in the fight against Sin. They cannot do it alone. They need women to join with them as sisters-in-arms.[18] They need people to remind them of their agency, empowered by Christ, and their call to fight against Sin in the church and the world. They need people who will fight alongside them. Society and the church desperately need what girls have to teach and the new creation they help form by telling their stories. This is the call for adults in ministry with adolescent girls, they must be allies in the fight.

Paul, like adolescent girls, knows that Sin is not relegated outside of the Christian community. In fact, his admonishments to the Roman Christians show that he sees the ways Christians in community can still be conscripted into Sin's army if they are not careful and intentional about their participation in Christ. Not only then do girls need sisters-in-arms who will help them confront the ways in which Sin is active in their experiences outside the church, they also need those who will acknowledge the

---

16. Groome, *Sharing Faith*, 18.

17. Parker, *Trouble Don't Last Always*, 15.

18. I chose to use this term to be consistent with reality as Paul expresses it and girls experience it. The present time is one of conflict between Sin and Grace, people are not neutral in this fight, nor are they removed from it. Brothers-in-arms is a military term for men who are fighting alongside each other. Girls need adults, and especially adult women, to fight the forces that threaten their humanity and wholeness alongside them as members together in the Body of Christ.

existence of and join their fight against Sin in the church. Through sisters-in-arms, churches can become "new creation hotspots" that encourage, shape, and support change outside of the church as well. Paul implores his readers and hearers in Rome to be instruments of righteousness in the ongoing war. Girls also need to be instruments of righteousness, too. They need help discerning how they can be a part of tackling Sin and being on God's side against Sin. They also need other women fighting with them and for them, their sisters-in-arms.

The girls whom I interviewed want to be active in this world and want to be inspired by their faith to do so. The critical eye they bring to the church can help hold the church accountable to be who they say they are. Girls can help identify where Sin is active in the church and can help the church to turn against it. The church needs this. They want things to change. They want to be a part of making changes in the church, their school, and society at large. Sharing and hearing the pictures girls paint in these small groups or partnerships with sisters-in-arms is only part of the task of embracing and engaging deeply with Paul's worldview.

Sisters-in-arms take the new creation brought forth in these times of sharing into the public space when they become allies with each other as girls develop and use their voice in public, from the pulpit to the halls of their schools to city council meetings. This is kin-dom building work. Adults can be powerful allies committed to encouraging girls' expressions of self, validating their experiences, and reserving judgment. Through hearing girls' stories with openness and love, girls can teach adults how to really see what is in them. The conversations I had were interviews, not pastoral conversations, yet still they were holy conversations.[19] This practice of listening facilitated their openness and encouraged them to continue to voice what they were experiencing and to continue to think through their beliefs even if they were not yet fully formed. Opening a safe space and inviting stories without judgment is one of the main tasks of educating into the new creation.

Old ways of knowing need to be broken apart, revealed as insufficient, damaging, and even misleading, and replaced by new ways of knowing and seeing the world. In *Almost Christian*, Kenda Creasy Dean writes about one of the important transformational effects of mission trips for youth. She

---

19. Baker and Mercer give voice to what can happen when listening deeply turns into a holy practice with young people even in the context of interviews in *Lives to Offer*, chapter 4.

writes, "The gift of these decentering encounters with "otherness"—the human other and the Divine other—is faithful *reflexivity*, a kind of self-awareness that allows us to momentarily view ourselves and others from a new vantage point as we watch God work."[20] She argues that this reflexivity is the spiritual practice of detachment, which "is liberation, freeing us from lesser allegiances that so we can entertain new possibilities that Christ presents for us and the world."[21] This is the kind of educational movement, which Dean also calls decentering, can happen, and needs to happen, right at home as girls learn to see their own paintings differently, to free their paintings from Sin. One need not leave home to encounter otherness because the world itself is other than girls have been led to believe.

This process of can be both painful and disorienting, as it is a break with the old and with the known. It is also not a neutral process; it is not that either way of seeing the painting is an appropriate way to form the imaginations of girls, adult sisters-in-arms, and the church. Decentering and seeing in a new way is part of the struggle between Grace and Sin. Old ways of knowing and seeing were under Sin; new ways are under Grace. These new ways are only freed through holy listening to each other's stories so that sisters-in-arms can help Paul's perspective shine new light on the lives of those who are telling them. For Paul, this shift in perspective happens through an encounter with Christ, something he also facilitates happening to the early Christians through his preaching and letters.[22] The revelation of Christ and the new perspective that comes with it is something one cannot make it happen for oneself, like baptism is occurs because of the power of the cross and is something that happens *to* a person. It is the job of the Christian community to offer opportunities for this shift to take place. When the church does not facilitate an encounter with Christ, the church is not functioning with the freedom in which it was formed.

When girls are helped to interpret their lives through Paul's theological lens, they can be freed from the trap of the old age. Living in the liminality of the new creation means seeing from the perspective of the new creation now, as it has broken into the present. When the experiences of girls are interpreted according to the new creation it is itself a practice of

---

20. Kenda Creasy Dean, *Almost Christian*, 159.

21. Ibid.

22. He describes his own encounter with Christ in Gal 1:15–16, though the more well-known account of his conversion was not reported by himself, but rather in the book of Acts.

the new creation, like the hearing of these stories is, as described above. When the new creation perspective is adopted for girls, their sisters-in-arms, and their churches, what is created is a new kind of community, the kind about which J. Louis Martyn wrote as being the corporately address-able, free community that is part of the new creation for which the universe is waiting. In that community, new ways of acting and being in the world are both expected and possible.

Girls cannot be in the world or in their churches in a new way on their own; they need a community to help them. Paul tells the Romans to participate, communally, in the world in a way that is consistent with who they are as baptized believers, those who have died to Sin and are alive in Christ. What he tells them to do is public and active, being enlisted in God's direct challenge to and defeat of Sin. As girls share their experiences and use their voices and bodies alongside other Christians' against dominant culture, they are doing what Paul asks of the believers in Rome. They are living as those who are alive in Christ. They are living in the new creation for which they wait, which is possible because Christ has been resurrected and they have been incorporated into him. The result of this kind of living has definite transformative consequences.

These areas are of common concern among scholars of Christian education and youth ministry—ability to articulate one's faith, theological interpretation of life, engagement with Scripture, and faithful action in the world—are the areas that Paul's writings and worldview can be especially helpful when employed in educating adolescent girls in the church.

A METHOD FOR MINISTRY WITH ADOLESCENT GIRLS

Christians need to see the world the way Paul does. They need the bifocal vision that J. Louis Martyn describes.[23] They need to see the old age, the present time, and the new creation, and to see the struggle between God and the powers of Sin and Death. Paul's letters and the perspective they both express and create in the listeners changes the way people see their own lives. Paul offers girls and women new lenses with which to observe and interpret each other's stories. With these lenses in place, girls and women can help their churches to see differently as well. With the support of their sisters-in-arms to use the new perspective gained by sharing their stories with each other in this interpretive community, girls are ready,

23. Martyn, *Theological Issues*, 284. Also referenced above in chapter 3.

along with their allies, to confront Sin in the church as a whole and seek for action in the world.

Like the prophetic imagination that Walter Brueggemann describes in his book *The Prophetic Imagination*, Paul's writings both critique and energize.[24] They show the world for what it is, revealing the powers of Sin and Death and revealing the power of God to conquer them.[25] They inspire hope by revealing, too, that the new creation is partially here, and that those who are in Christ are already in the new creation, able to see and act from a place of freedom and with the power of Grace. Adolescent girls are gifted with a critical eye and with passion.[26] Girls are uniquely positioned to join in naming the world in a way that does what Paul's naming of the world does: describe reality as it is and produce hope. Educating into the new creation is about calling the world what it is and about proclaiming the death of Sin in the lived realities of those who are in Christ.

Paul writes that believers can align themselves with Sin or with God now that they are free from being enslaved to Sin. Speaking their lives out from the silence that the culture in the United States inflicts on them is an act of resistance on the part of adolescent girls. A community of sister-in-arms, girls and women together, inviting stories, hearing them, and interpreting them according to Paul's worldview is an act of communal resistance to and fight against Sin. Sin seeks to enlist their help in perpetuating their own oppression in society and the church. When these sisters-in-arms take these stories into their churches, which are often unknowingly siding with Sin in their treatment of girls, it is an act of not only resistance but also powerful

---

24. Brueggemann, *The Prophetic Imagination*, 13.

25. Christian education scholar Richard Osmer also uses Paul as a resource for Christian education in the church, and he looks to J. Louis Martyn's explanation of Paul's bifocal vision as a helpful way to describe what Paul hopes his hearers will understand from his ministry and letters. However, Osmer argues that the most useful take away from what he calls Paul's teaching ministry is discernment. "At the heart of Paul's understanding of discernment is learning how to live and think eschatologically, discerning the circumstances of everyday life in the light of God's promised future for creation." Osmer, *The Teaching Ministry of Congregations*, 44. Osmer fails to understand the nature of Paul's worldview. For Paul it is not about discernment or thinking, it is about seeing the world for what it is. This happens through the revelation of Christ, which happens not through thinking or a spiritual practice of discernment but through the Christ event being made present resulting in believers seeing themselves as part of a new body. To know the world for what it is, to know from the new creation, is the work of Christ, aided by the power of Paul's words and the mystery of baptism.

26. Kenda Creasy Dean argues that passion is a hallmark of adolescence. See *Practicing Passion*, especially Introduction and chapter 1.

act of Grace. The church participates in destroying Sin by welcoming Grace when it actively asks for girls' stories, learns from them, and support girls in tangible changes in and outside the church as a result. This kind of church knows itself, the time in which we live, its members, and the whole world from new creation perspective. They have been taught to see reality differently. They have been taught to see the world for what it is, to seen Sin for what it is, and to see Grace for what it is—the power of the new creation.

Listen

Like other liberative pedagogies, perhaps most famously Paulo Freire in *Pedagogy of the Oppressed*, I begin with lived experience in this model of Pauline liberative Christian education, educating into the new creation. As noted above, when I asked these girls if they had been asked these kinds of questions before, they mainly responded in the negative.[27] Educating into the new creation involves first and foremost giving space for and encouragement to girls so that they become articulate by taking them seriously and by listening deeply to them. If girls are to be welcomed into the Body of Christ that is the church, they must be welcomed with their voices and experiences, not in spite of them and not with exceptions built into the invitation. Inviting girls to share their stories in their churches and welcoming those stories as holy is a challenge for churches who are accustomed to ministry with young people involving only transfer of information about Christianity and training in morals.

Youth ministries often fail to honor the fact that youth have much to teach to their churches about themselves and about the practice of Christian faith in today's world. Participating in the new creation that can come through the sharing and receiving of girls' stories will empower girls to take their voices beyond their snaps, Facebook timelines, Twitter feeds, and youth rooms. When girls take their voices to the church, they can also be empowered and encouraged to take their voices to society. An empowering new creation begun with hearing girls to speech in the church will lead

---

27. This is consistent with the findings of the NSYR (Smith and Denton, *Soul Searching*, 267), the research conducted by Joyce Mercer with adolescent girls at Emory School of Theology's Youth Theological Initiative (Mercer, *Girltalk/Godtalk*, xx), and the theoretical background to Dori Baker's religious education model (Baker, *Doing Girlfriend Theology*, especially chapter one).

to girls developing a public voice and public action, because God's new creation consists of just that, a changed world.

Welcoming stories and being taught by them can be as simple as meeting with a small group of girls and adult women around the table at a coffee shop, asking questions about life, hopes, disappointments, and faith, and listening deeply for the answers. During the group interviews, I sometimes became a witness to the holy conversation between Christian friends as I stopped asking questions and observed the conversation flow between the girls. They challenged each other, affirmed each other, and asked questions of each other. Adolescent girls have stories to tell. They have pictures to paint for those who will listen; and they need support when their stories are not welcomed as or trusted to be the holy stories they are.

At age 12, Martin Pistorius entered a vegetative state for reasons unknown to his doctors. For the next 12 years, his family cared for him, assuming that in that state he was completely unaware of what was going on around him. He was not—he began to wake up by the age of 14 or 15. National Public Radio's *All Things Considered* quotes Pistorius as saying "Everyone was so used to me not being there that they didn't notice when I began to be present again."[28] Adults are used to assuming that youth have nothing to teach adults and have nothing to share with adults. Adults in church often assume, even if implicitly or unconsciously, that adolescents should be only recipients of the knowledge and experience of adults. Practical theologian Mary McClintock Fulkerson calls the not-seeing of other people "obliviousness."[29] She observes that this obliviousness is "not primarily intentional but reflexive. As such, it occurs on an experiential continuum ranging from benign to a subconscious or repressed protection of power."[30] Part of the perspectival shift needed in the church as a whole is to see youth, to notice and rebel against its own obliviousness, whether it is benign or an exercise of power over the youth. Education into the new creation is education for the church as a whole about the importance and value of youth and what they can contribute to the church and the church's mission in the world.

---

28. Lulu Miller, "Trapped in his body for 12 years a man breaks free," *National Public Radio*, January 9, 2015, http://www.npr.org/blogs/health/2015/01/09/376084137/trapped-in-his-body-for-12-years-a-man-breaks-free.

29. McClintock Fulkerson, *Places of Redemption*, 18.

30. Ibid., 19.

Girls need the help of their sisters-in-arms in order for them and their stories to be noticed and welcomed into the faith community. The church is so used to girls not being there that without these sisters-in-arms being a kind of mediator between the girls and the rest of the church, they will not notice when girls do begin to be present. Girls need adult allies to enable other adults see them.

McClintock Fulkerson argues that seeing others and being seen by others in the community of faith is essential. She writes, "What is needed to counter the diminishment and harm associated with obliviousness is *a place to appear*, a place to be seen, to be recognized and to recognize the other. Being seen and heard by others, being acknowledged by others—these are said to be essential to the political life; my point is that they are also essential to a community of faith as an honoring of the shared image of God."[31] The church needs to be a place to appear for adolescent girls, both for the benefit of the girls and for the benefit of the church. Listening deeply to the lives of adolescent girls is about hearing them into their full humanity. Listening in this way, asking for stories, being open to hearing whatever experiences the girls have—the beautiful and the broken—is a way to acknowledge, welcome, and encourage them to embrace their full humanity. As adult sisters-in-arms share their own stories with adolescent girls, girls will be all the more fully welcomed into the church, as those who have experienced holy conversation and sharing with other members of the Body.

Girls also need to be invited into the full life of the church with their full selves. Girls should preach from the pulpit. Girls should serve on committees in ways that value their presence and ideas, not tokenize or patronize them. Girls should be teaching others—adults and children and each other—in Sunday school classes. Girls should be asked about what they see as the most important concerns of our time. Girls should help plan worship. There will, undoubtedly, be instances in which the congregation will not be receptive to stories girls tell, will judge these stories with an "old age" knowing, or will be uncertain of how to respond to the new truths they bring to light.

Sisters-in-arms are allies in the challenge of bringing girls and their lives into the Body of Christ. When Tay was criticized for preaching about cutting, she needed a trusted adult woman with whom she had already shared her story to stand up for her. This adult could have shown the church how their

---

31. Ibid., 21, italics original.

response was in line with Sin rather than with Grace. When girls hear members of churches criticizing their dress, girls need to have trusted women to whom they can bring this problem and find help in addressing it.

The challenges that girls face, including the dehumanizing systems and situations that threaten them, are very real. They are part of the ongoing struggle of the present time, waiting for final obliteration when the new creation is completely birthed into the world at the eschaton. Because they are real and really threaten a young person's humanity, each young person needs others, including adults, to take them seriously and in partnership with Christ work to destroy those threats.

Reading Paul

Paul's letters are both pedagogical and inspirational. He trusts that by writing these letters, along with connecting in person with these fledgling Christian communities, he will be able to evoke a new perspective on the world in those communities. Part of his pedagogical strategy is to tell his listeners about the world as he sees it. By showing them the signs of the present time, the powers of the old age, and the coming of the new creation, they, too, begin to see their churches and their lives in this way. He uses powerful and descriptive language to help the readers of his letters see the way he does. He paints a vivid picture of the present time and the struggle taking place. The language he uses changes the way people hear and see so that in the painting he also teaches them how to see the world around them for what it really is.

Learning how to see through Paul's lens is a challenge. This challenge is amplified because it is not only about seeing, it includes living in a new way in response. Churches, including both adults and youth in them, need to hear and interpret Paul's words in a new way if his words are to have the transformative power that they had when Paul first wrote them. Paul has been interpreted to churches, including to youth, without taking his worldview into consideration. Biblical language is difficult for many in the church to listen to with openness and understanding. The church as a history of interpretation and curriculum around that interpretation that has been used for so long that it is difficult to hear Paul in a new way. Kenda Creasy Dean says that teaching the Christian tradition to young people is translation, similar to translating Scripture into the languages people speak as part of mission work.[32] She writes that "Translation requires communities that embody the tradition in three-dimensional form, and adults who can connect these traditions to daily life . . ."[33] Sisters-in-arms, those who are adolescent and those who are adult, need to listen to Paul's words and let them transform the way they see the world. The letters Paul writes cannot do what they were designed to do unless they are given space to perform as they did in the first century. Sisters-in-arms have a new task; they must be diligent in getting to know Paul's worldview and adopt his lens for interpreting their own stories. Sisters-in-arms, both youth and adults, will be the ones going out into the mission field of their own churches tasked with translating Paul to those who think they know him and who in reality don't.

Until now, the church has not been a purveyor of Paul's worldview and therefore has not characterized struggles and sufferings in light of what time it is. Pastors and youth ministers have read Paul without awareness to the real struggle about which he writes. Faithful congregants have heard Paul's words of warning or moralistic checklists and have either ignored them or used them as a weapon against freedom. Girls have not had the opportunity to see the world for what it is; they have not been taught to do so. Neither have those adults who would be sisters-in-arms had this opportunity.

Girls need to hear Paul's letters in a new way. So, too, do adults who intend to be allies to our teenage girls. We need to hear Paul's words that identify the anti-God powers and speak confidently of the promise of their defeat in the time that is to come. We need to hear Paul's words telling us how we can act differently now because we are in Christ, not because we have a moralistic checklist to follow, but because we are free and far more powerful together in Christ than we ever thought possible. We need Paul to incite all of us to action, just as he did for the first hearers of his letters.

Paul's letters were meant to be read aloud, not in a monotonous reverent tone, but as passionate discourse that not only said something but did something.[34] The way that we read Paul's letters in worship, youth group, Sunday school, or small groups of sisters-in-arms, matters. We need to read his words aloud, tuning into his perspective to guide the way that we read and emphasize. If Scripture seems somehow old, out of touch, and inaccessible in the spaces in which we encounter it, we need to encounter it

32. Dean, *Almost Christian*, 116.

33. Ibid., 117.

34. See the discussion on p. 111 for more on this concept.

elsewhere. Paul's diagnosis of the time in which we are living is not stale. It is vibrant and colorful. It is bright and clear. Our ears are yearning to hear it. When we hear Paul's insistence that we become weapons of righteousness, and not weapons of Sin with an awareness to his worldview, we can clearly hear that this calls us to act to dismantle racism, sexism, sizeism, and homophobia because we know that to do otherwise is to fight on the side of Sin, even to be used by Sin against God and the freedom God gives people in Christ. Paul's call to act in this way inspires us to seek possibilities for our action on the side of God instead. Moreover, we answer this call as a community because we realize that Paul is not calling individuals, he is calling individuals-in-the-Body-of Christ. We are in this fight together with our sisters-in-arms and our churches; together with Christ. We act with the power of Grace and even as weapons of Grace in the fight. Somehow "grace" has come to mean something far less potent than Paul envisioned it as. Grace is what killed Death on the cross. Grace is what we bear with us when we confront the forces that threaten our humanity and overwhelm our agency. Paul trusted that his words could convey power in his absence, this is what his letters were intended to do and what they did. These same words can convey power for us in the 21st century, too. Educating into the new creation, then, is a process of engaging with Paul's words and with the text of lived experience.

Question Posing

As sisters-in-arms help each other interpret their stories in light of Paul's worldview and change the way they see the world, intentional ways of asking questions of the stories shared will help guide girls and women to that interpretation and new perspective. In fact, these same questions can be used in reading Paul's own letters to begin to hear the perspective he held operating underneath the words. Whether reading a letter of Paul or listening to an adolescent girl share about her life, these questions can guide the interpretation and offer a new lens for seeing their lives in real time. These questions can teach us how to see what has been "painted." These questions, and the answers they elicit can guide the translation. Adult women who want to be sisters-in-arms with adolescent girls need to work through these questions in conversations with each other to guide their understanding of their own stories, too. The fact is that, because of how Sin limits our perspective and because of how Paul has been used throughout Christian history, we cannot see even our own paintings clearly. These questions can help sisters-in-arms, as a community of girls and women working together to paint their stories and teach each other how to see them, continually to interpret their stories while reflecting on the past and while processing their current lived experience.

- What is going on in this story?
- Where is the power of Sin in this story?
- Where is the grace of God in this story?
- Where is God in this story? Is there an invitation from God to you in this story?
- In what way is Sin trying to use you for its purpose in this story?
- In what way is the Spirit empowering you to fight against Sin in this story?
- In what way can your community of sisters-in-arms come to your defense against Sin in this story?
- What is the promise of God present in this story? Where is the hope that we can count on?
- What will help you maintain your hope in that promise being fulfilled?
- How can we (your sisters-in-arms, peers, church) help you keep your hope and fight against Sin?

None of these questions is about how "good" or "bad", "sinful" or "grace-filled" the actors in the story are in their actions, perceptions, thinking, or feeling. The emphasis from a new creation perspective is that the human agent is free in Christ to side with God against Sin and Death. That freedom is not a moral choice, but rather a reality created by the grace of God enacted in Christ's work on the cross. Seeing themselves as free in Christ and empowering them to live into that freedom is what happens when a girl knows the world from the new creation perspective and is supported by her sisters-in-arms who are seeking the same freedom. Girls can use their developing critical thinking skills as they examine their lives. In a way, this process enables girls to have a "decentering encounter" with their own stories. Because seeing the way Paul does means acting with God against Sin, possibilities for action are discernable through this question-posing. This is the righteous action to which the Body of Christ is called and in which it is free to participate with God.

Naming the Powers

Paul understood the power of naming the reality of one's world and one's experience in it. Paul's letters were addressed to communities gathered to re-present Christ in the world. They were intended to be read aloud and to transform those who listened. Paul understood that when Jesus died on the cross and then rose from the dead, a death knell for power of Sin was sounded. On the cross, the power of Sin was defeated, even as the battle against it in the present liminal time continues to rage. New Testament scholar Alexandra Brown suggests that when Paul writes about the cross, which gets proclaimed through the reading of his letters to the gathered Christians, he moves his audience from old age knowing to new creation knowing.[35] His writing makes something happen. When Paul paints the picture of the cross, the salvific event happens again in the present. The power of Sin is broken on the cross, again and again as the cross is powerfully preached and made present in the ears of the hearers. The language of the cross exposes the situation for what it is and frees those who are oppressed by it. How this happens for Paul can give us insight into how we as sisters- and brothers-in-arms can make it happen with the girls in our communities today.

In many of Paul's letters, he calls his readers and hearers to become like him.[36] In what way Paul is calling for mimicry is up for debate, but it is clear that he intends to be a teacher through his writing. He can offer adult sisters-in-arms who are teachers and advocates for adolescent girls in their churches an example of how to help others see in a new way. This is what he does with his letters. Having experienced a transformative revelation of Christ in his life that shifted his perspective, Paul sets out mediate transformation for others. In addition to whatever preaching, teaching, and baptizing Paul practiced in his visits to newly forming Christian communities, his letters remind his hearers of the Gospel and make the Christ event present again through his written word, which was proclaimed to the communities in his absence. His letters offered a "decentering encounter" that made Christ present and changed the way people saw their world and understood

---

35. Brown, *Cross and Human Transformation*, 14.

36. For example, 1 Corinthians 4:16, Galatians 4:12, Philippians 3:17.

their lives. The gospel of Christ is proclaimed in Romans (and his other letters) and Christ is revealed breaking into their present time and through the words Paul pens. Adult sisters-in-arms can employ Paul's own pedagogy by exposing power of Sin, and its partners, as the powers they are, just like Paul does in his letters.

In his letters, Paul tells people again and again what time it is and what the powers are. He describes their world to them explicitly. He also tells them who they are in this world, reminding them that they are in Christ and empowered in their actions because they live Christ's life now. He uses imperative statements to call his readers and hearers to action in the world on the side of God. Sometimes girls will need their sisters-in-arms to describe what the world looks like through Paul's lens. Question-posing and engaging critical thinking will not be enough. Sometimes sister-in-arms will need to be more instructive or didactic rather than relying on girls' realizing through their own investigation of their stories. Girls will need to be told where Sin is located when they cannot see it for themselves even with the careful question-posing exploration as outlined above. They will need to be told what righteous action against Sin can look like. Paul does this in his letters, too. And just like Paul, sisters-in-arms using the imperative to tell people what action they should do prayerfully, with commitment and connection to the folks they are telling to act, and with the confidence that these actions are a part of working with God in the world. They can do so because Christ has already been revealed to them.

Modeling Perspective

Another way Paul teaches with his letters is by sharing about his own life and his own experience of Christ. He tells them who he is and how his perspective was changed, in addition to sharing what that new perspective is. Girls may find it easier to see from a new creation perspective by hearing someone else's story interpreted in this way before trying to interpret their own stories. Adult sisters-in-arms can model new creation perspective and how they came to see that way as they tell their own stories and interpret them for the girls with whom they are allies.

Movies, memes, current events, song lyrics, advertisements, and television shows are also excellent ways to practice interpreting the world based on Paul's worldview. The goal is to help girls interpret their own lives in this way, but sometimes an easier entry point is to practice on someone else's story. Paul tells his own story to prove to his audience how different life is when Christ is revealed. Our stories are powerful. Sharing them is a powerful pedagogical tool.

Interpretation of lived stories from the new creation perspective is not something that happens on one's own. Sisters-in-arms need a community of co-interpreters, and serve as that for each other. Girls and women need sisters who will model a new creation perspective for them, these examples become the proof that seeing in a new way makes life different. The guilt, remorse, and low self-esteem that comes from interpreting the world and our place in it from the old age perspective run deeply and are pervasive, as is the autonomous individualism of the culture of the United States. Helping girls to see the powers at work in the world will be liberating from Sin and transformative. Helping girls to see that this change is real for their sisters-in-arms is part of the liberation. In fact, helping others see the world for what it really is part of the righteous action that follows from being aligned with Grace instead of Sin. This perspective shift, a conversion of how one sees and knows the world, happens through other members of the Body of Christ, through the movement of the Holy Spirit, and through God's own self-revelation, just as it happened in the first century. Paul teaches people how to see the world differently and models that change in his own life. Sisters-in-arms are called to mimic Paul's pedagogy in their own modeling with and for each other.

Girls can be co-interpreters of each other's stories and of adult sisters'-in-arms stories. Adult sisters-in-arms need the critical eye of girls as they seek to continue to see from new creation perspective. The power of Sin is so strong that it will attempt to maintain old age knowing; part of the struggle of the present time to see Sin at all. A community of co-interpreters solidly grounded in and living from their own identity in Christ can help focus each other's eyes so they can see reality. Like Paul, they can tell each other that they are free to act differently than the world under Sin expects. They, too, can show each other how to avoid being enlisted into the force that is amassing on the side of Sin.

A Call to Arms

Members of the Body of Christ are the weapons God uses to defeat the powers of Sin and Death that threaten these girls' humanity. Allies, sisters – and brothers-in-arms, are armed with the power of Grace, the Spirit of Christ, the awareness of where Sin is active, and the freedom to act righteously in a time where Sin is still powerfully deceiving and confining people who do not yet have the bifocal vision those who are in Christ do. Fighting against Sin is fighting for the liberation of adolescent girls.

There are several ways that Sin is active in this world, the stories with which I was entrusted for this project show several. It seems that at the root of the ways these girls experienced Sin inside and outside of the church was in relationship to their bodies. Everyone has a body. Most of the girls I spoke with were conflicted over whether this was a good or bad thing because of how their bodies have been interpreted to them, often because of the fact that their bodies are female. When girls are taught, whether explicitly or implicitly that their bodies are sinful or cause sin in others by being sexually tempting, they will inevitably feel badly about themselves for the body they have. Seeing the world differently means seeing that Sin is clearly at work in churches and in our American culture as evidenced by the way that girls' bodies are sexualized, feared, and shamed. Because Sin is still at work everywhere, even in churches, it is imperative for believers to fight against Sin together, even when it manifests in the Christian community. Paul does not devalue the body, nor does he see the human body as the source of unrighteous action. Sin is always to blame. Focusing on the body, on any body, distracts from rooting out Sin. The culture of the United States has often focused on the female body as a target of marketing and of control. Not only is this some of the ways sexism is part of the make-up of this country, it is also part of the heterosexism and heteronormativity of it. Girls' value is often equated with how they look, a message that is well-received by the time a girl reaches adolescence. Christian girls are also given two opposing messages—they are to be attractive, and yet being too attractive means they are causing someone else to sin. They are to date the right kind of boy and prepare for the right kind of Christian man to whom they will someday be married.

The girls I interviewed are not only female bodies and differently-sized bodies, they are also marked by their race and culture. Immigrant girls and first generation American girls struggle with feeling as if they do not fit with their families or with the culture in this country. They are aware that expectations placed on them by their communities and families are different than those placed on peers whose families and communities are from this country. Girls who are bilingual are marked by accents. Race is a powerful social construct that affects the way these girls interact with the world around them and the way the world interacts with them. Girls like Sam struggle to know what their race means to themselves and others when they are parented by those of another race. Girls like Sadie are aware of their white privilege but unsure about what to do about it beyond feeling guilty. Girls like Raven and Monica give voice to the explicit ways racism against Black bodies shows up in their lives and in the ways their neighborhoods and neighbors are treated by individuals and society as a whole. There is a lot to fight against; Sin is prevalent. But it is not as powerful as Grace.

Many models of Christian education call for action, educating into the new creation does as well, because this is fundamental to Paul's perspective. As he clearly states in Romans, members of the Body of Christ are called to be weapons of righteousness in the fight against Sin. This happens in concrete living in the in-between time and is, by necessity, something the community does together. Sin's power can be seen in racism, sexism, sizism, and homophobia. Evelyn Parker acknowledges some of these same structures and systems of our society and emphasizes social economic systems as well. She does not however, interpret these as the power of Sin in the way that Paul's worldview pushes us. Parker writes, "Emancipatory hope is expectation that the forms of hegemonic relations—race, class, and gender dominance—will be toppled, and to have emancipatory hope is to acknowledge one's personal agency in God's vision for human equality."[37] What Parker calls "hegemonic relations" are part of how Sin in at work in this world. They will indeed be toppled. However, in a Pauline perspective, it does not happen through personal agency, rather it happens through one's personal agency being freed by being in Christ and by living and acting as an indivisible part of Christ's body now. God's vision is for human equality; this is clear in other of Paul's writings as well (for example, 1 Corinthians 12, Galatians 3). A freed human agent, who is not autonomous but instead deeply and indivisibly connect to others in the Body, as the Body, can act in powerful ways that continue to fight against and liberate others from the power of Sin as it operates in our present time.

HOPE THAT IS SEEN IS NOT HOPE

In revisiting two stories from this project, I offer example of how interpreting them according to Paul's worldview is a valuable tool in helping girls see their power and freedom in the situations expressed, and offers

37. Parker, *Trouble Don't Last Always*, 11.

opportunities for sisters-in-arms to fight against the powers Paul's perspective reveals.

In chapter 2, I shared the following story from Monica:

> But the only time, like, something like that ever happened was I think when I took a train for the first time by myself . . . only, like, 2 stops and like, I sat next to this guy and he called me "the n-word." And I was like, I was so taken back, like I didn't know. I think I told Mommy, I don't, it just didn't occur to me how like crazy it was. I just I was so confused because, like, I had never heard,' cause I don't use the word. I don't, I don't hear people, well, at the time I didn't really hear people saying it cause, like, I [had gone to] a really like a close-knit Catholic school going into public school, so that in itself was just like a . . . shock. And then for something like that to happen. And the people just stared at me for like 2 stops. And I was just like, "Did he expect me to, did they expect me to, like, say something? Should I have said something? Or what?"

Interpreting Monica's story from a new creation way of knowing begins with understanding that in this present time, suffering is expected. The fact that there is hatred, racism, and a man verbally attacking a girl on the subway is proof that, at this time, Sin is still an active power. Monica mentioning that her close-knit Catholic school helped to protect her from this kind of hatred shows that even in this time in which we wait for the new creation, a Christian community might be able to give us the freedom to live in a hate-free space. That this was a shock to Monica shows some righteousness breaking in; the old age is not the only way to define the time. No one came to help Monica, no one spoke against the man for using the hate speech he did; in fact, Monica felt like the people on the train expected her to do something. She questions herself and her own reaction. Monica felt alone and as a victim with no power; not only because of the power of the word the man on the train used, but also because she was not armed to fight against that power, that word, that man. The man who called her "the n-word" and other people on the subway became partners with Sin, which exposed itself as racism. Interpreting the story like this helps Monica see that she was not at fault for not responding. Had her community (her Catholic school) provided her not only with a safe space but also with weapons to fight against Sin in that kind of situation, she may have been able to respond differently, but this is not her fault. In fact, Sin is at work in her community, attempting to prevent its members from using each other and the tools of Grace to dismantle Sin.

Grace is present in Monica's knowing that this was not acceptable. Grace is present in her recognizing her own shock. Grace is present in that she was able to share this experience with a trusted ally, her mother. The call to arms for her peer and adult sisters-in-arms is to also join with Grace in disarming Sin. If the interview where Monica told this story was instead a small group of girls and women gathered for the purpose of sharing stories in order to interpret them according to Paul's worldview, part of the task would be to discern action to take on the side of God, and then to do that action together as members of Christ's Body. Sin is using the people on that train as instruments in its war against Grace. These people, too, need to be freed from Sin, and freed from sinning by participating in racism and in complicity with racism. Paulo Friere wrote that oppressors lose their humanity when they dehumanize others.[38] Sin is holding the man on the train captive and the silent bystanders captive. Monica, with the alliance of her sisters-in-arms and her church can be freed herself and can free others. Monica needs support as she confronts these situations, attempts to make sense of them, and finds empowerment instead of paralyzing shock and self-doubt. A group of sisters-in-arms who have heard Monica to speak this story and helped her interpret it can help Monica share with the rest of the church and discern together action the community can take in response to her experience. Their church can evaluate ways they have been failing to act as a weapon against Sin and find ways to change their alliance to be with God and righteous action instead. Her church misses the opportunity to become instruments of God against Sin if they miss hearing her story and discerning a course of action that responds to it. Just as Paul tells the hearers of his letters to be instruments of righteousness to live new lives dead to death, so, too, can sisters-in-arms and a community of those open to hearing Monica's story call Monica and each other to act in righteousness knowing that Sin is not in control of this world. Self-doubt and shock need not be the way this story ends. Instead, this story, shared in a community of co-interpreting sisters-in-arms, can lead to action on the part of Monica and her community, knowing that Sin expressed in racism against a teenage girl on the train will be defeated, and they are a part of making that happen. I imagine, for example, the possibility that Monica has partners from her church who will ride the train with her every day now so she is not alone. These partners will be ready to stand up against hate speech should it be directed toward Monica or anyone else on the train. Maybe the church can

38. Freire, *Pedagogy of the Oppressed*, 56.

hold trainings for what to do when someone is threatened by racism. Maybe the church partners with a neighboring church with majority white members who learn how it is their job to be on the train and speak against other white people who threaten people of color. There are creative possibilities for action on the side of God against Sin in response to the sharing of Monica's story and seeing Sin and Grace for what they are in it.

Genevieve told a story about how she learned from her brothers and other boys in her youth group that she should be sure cover up her body well if she is going to attract the right kind of Christian man. This is a clear example of the confusion about the need to both attract a guy and yet not be too attractive, all based on how she chooses to present her body. She shared this story:

> You see these girls walking around in the tank tops but they cut all the way down to like one inch [above the waist on the side] . . . And they wear sports bras. So you see the sports bra or the normal bra and then you have all this skin down here and it's just like you're every day clothes! Like, I never really thought about it too much, but then last year [on the work mission trip], um, I had this really in depth talk with my brothers and the other guys in the youth group and they were like, "It's so difficult! Because we're trying to be good Christian guys but these girls . . . " Even just like seeing the bra is just like enough to be like, "that's temptation!" So I have been very aware of the fact that it is tough for guys who want to be good because I figure the kind of guy that I want to end up is going to be like my brothers or like these other boys and they say they don't like it when the girls tempt them so I'm like, "Alright, well." . . . it's just kind of, it makes it easier for me to know that if I do that I'm going to attract that kind of guy that I don't want so I'm not going to do that. I'm going to dress the way I want to dress and it's, I think it's not too tempting.

On the one hand, she clearly wants to attract a Christian guy, though she expects this to happen in some way controlled by God. On the other hand, in order to attract the right kind of guy, she knows she cannot dress like the girls who show their bras at work camp because these boys have told her that it prevents them from being good Christian guys. In other words, her clothing choice determines whether the boys she attracts are good Christians or not. She is the cause of boys who are trying to be good Christians failing to do so.

Paul would support Genevieve's feeling of responsibility toward her fellow brothers in Christ. However, the fact that they and she believe that it is the female body that causes sinning is not something with which he would agree. It is not Genevieve's body that is the cause of sinning, rather it is Sin itself. In this example, Sin is working to convince boys that girls' bodies are the problem. Sin is working to equate girls' worth with how their bodies are received by others, especially boys. Sin is working to convince Genevieve that her body causes sinfulness in others, and that she is responsible for making that not happen. She ended her story with the statement, "I'm going to dress the way I want to dress and it's, I think it's not too tempting." On the one hand, the boys in her youth group have given her permission to not dress the way that she sees other girls dressing. This in itself might be liberative. She might be struggling to know that it is a reasonable choice for an adolescent girls to cover herself. She has permission to dress more conservatively and trust that she will still be able to attract the right kind of guy. This can certainly be seen as positive: she is given an alternative to the media's expectation that girls should dress their bodies in ways that capitalize on sexual appeal. Because of this conversation, she knows that displaying her body in a way that makes her uncomfortable is not the way to attract the kind of man she knows she wants to attract. On the other hand, she is also not convinced that it is possible to dress in a way that does not cause guys to sin. Her statement, "I think it's not too tempting" shows that she is uncertain, but she imagines it is still at least somewhat tempting. It is also the case that Genevieve, her brothers, and the other boys she was talking with from her youth group are making judgments about the girls who dress in such a way that shows their bras. They do not leave space for the possibility that it can be a liberative choice on the part of girls to dress however they want, even if their bra is showing. What if Genevieve did want to dress so that her bra showed? Maybe because it is hot working on construction in the summer and it is permissible for boys to take off their shirts but not girls. Maybe because she thinks it's cute. Maybe because her body is powerful and she celebrates it. In the way Genevieve interprets this story, that choice is not available to her even if she did want it because it would be sinful to do so.

The messages girls receive about their bodies and how they are related to sin exhibit "old age knowing." Therefore, a call to arms against the power of Sin and how it is effecting girls' perception and acceptance (or rejection) of their bodies is needed. Seeing and knowing the world for what it really is reveals the power of Sin at work in how the boys see themselves in relation to girls, in girls seeking to get guys' attention by dressing in revealing ways, in girls thinking their bodies are only a tool for attracting guys, in girls who are unable to choose their clothing without it being perceived as a message to guys, and in Genevieve's uncertainty that her body can be anything other than tempting. Were Genevieve's story heard by a group of sisters-in-arms, her assumptions about herself and her body would be exposed as one of Sin's tactic. The entire church needs education about how girls' bodies are unconsciously and consciously perceived by members of the community. The church is called to arms against the exploitation of girls' bodies, the interpretations of their bodies as sinful, and the ways that boys perceive themselves as captive to their own sexual interest. The possibilities for action on the part of the church as weapons of righteous against Sin are many. Genevieve with the help of her sisters-in-arms might be able to come up with a ritual that blesses their bodies and wrests it away from the interpretations of sinfulness. Maybe girls in the church can be led through activities that celebrate all their bodies are and do. Maybe the church can begin a letter writing campaign to industries that are particularly damaging in perpetuating the view that girls' bodies are sinful and tempting—maybe even especially to Christian publishing houses who do this through their curriculum, versions of the Bible, and devotional material. Knowing according to the new creation includes seeing the teenage girl body as good, as a place where Grace can be revealed, as a source of strength and action against Sin. Moreover, the desire for intimacy is not sinful. Boys do not need to be protected from it, girls do not need to be held responsible for it.

Through the sharing and interpretation of this story with sisters-in-arms and then with the whole church through sisters-in-arms acting as allies with Genevieve, the community as a whole would be invited to discern righteous action against how girls and boys relate to and understand the teenage girl body. Genevieve might be free from seeing her body as inherently sinful and the church can act in ways that free others from that damaging assumption.

Paul ends his eighth chapter in the letter to the Romans writing about hope and confidence. We wait with patience for what we know is coming but is not yet here. We trust that the Spirit intercedes on our behalf because we are in Christ. And we know, without a doubt, that nothing can separate us from the love of God in Christ, no matter how strong the power of Sin appears. Having dealt with Sin so completely in this chapter of Romans, Paul does not discuss it as a power any further in the letter. Paul knows that although the new creation is yet to fully be born, the fact that it is inevitably on its way, as the labor pains of creation clearly indicate, means that our hope rests firm in its impending arrival. Our participation in Christ's death and resurrection proves that we who are in Christ can operate now in the power of Grace and work along with Grace against the aspects of Sin that remain in this liminal time and space.

The church benefits from being changed by the stories that adolescent girls bring with them as they are truly and fully welcomed into the church. When Sadie describes the subway ride when her fear of being attacked by a man was confronted with the powerful presence of the Spirit. She is describing an encounter with the Holy. She went from paralyzing fear to comfort, even joy, and then to movement off the train and into her school day. She felt the presence of God and knew, for the first time, that God was real and involved in her life. Her story has enriched my life. I felt her fear when the boy from her youth group tried to force physical intimacy with her. I felt anger that she judged her fear as unnecessary since she "wasn't actually raped." I felt relief that she was able to get away from him. I felt peace when she curled up in her father's lap and told her mother what had happened. I again felt her fear as she realized she was on a stopped train car with only one other person, a man. And when she told me about the seats filling with smiling faces and a presence settling on her fearful heart, I, too, experienced the presence of God.

Sadie's story both said something to me and did something in me as I experienced the power of God to conquer Sin. Sadie offered critique and energy, pain and hope. She is a prophet and an instrument of God. She described the current contested time where a boy invades her space and tries to force intimacy, creating deep fear in her about men and boys. She experienced the Spirit filling the subway seats, giving her confidence and hope, and releasing her from paralyzing fear so that she could get up from her seat and enter her school day. Sadie's church community and the support of her parents in a scary and difficult time formed her into being receptive to the Spirit when it came, transforming a moment of deep fear into a moment of holiness.

As we wait for the new creation, stories like Sadie's show us that it is both on its way and already here. As adults who are called to minister alongside adolescent girls in this present time, it is in hope that we wait for that new creation to fully be here. We wait, along with these girls, for a time when Sadie is not attacked by a friend and when she does not have good reason to fear for her safety on the subway—when Sin is not at all present. We wait patiently, not because the struggles of the present time are not real or should not be confronted, but because we know with absolute certainty that these struggles will end. Sin does not and cannot win. We wait patiently knowing we are called and empowered to act in righteousness against Sin now. We wait patiently because of our certainty in the future that is resurrection and the complete and utter defeat of Sin. We wait patiently because girls like Sadie, and the other 24 girls with whom I spoke live lives that can do for the church community now what Paul's letters did then—show us the way the world is and facilitate the Spirit in producing hope through this new way of perceiving and acting in the world.

chapter 5

AN EPISTLE TO ADOLESCENT GIRLS
AND THEIR CHURCHES

A letter to the churches of Jesus Christ, from a United Methodist pastor in the United States who is also a professor, scholar, and advocate for young people,

Some of you I may know, some of you I don't. Some of you I may meet one day. But whether I know you personally or not, I believe that you are my brothers and sisters in the Body of Christ. I was baptized into the United Methodist Church as a teenager, after experiencing Christ on a youth group retreat. I believe that in that moment, God revealed Jesus to me as the one from whom I would never be separated. My journey toward being a Christian is lifelong process. I am always learning and growing closer to God through Jesus and am guided by the Holy Spirit. So as your sister in Christ, who has experienced the in-breaking love of God and is always searching for how to become more closely aligned with God's promise and hope for this, God's world, I write to you. Not as someone who has it all together or is a better Christian than any of you, just as someone who cares deeply about God and our church. Someone who knows what it is like to desperately want the kindom of God to be here already so all the pain, hatred, and struggle can be over.

I know you have a lot going on. I know you are worried about social issues in our country. You are worried about politicians and legislations. You are worried about climate change, or you are worried about how many people are (not) worried about climate change. You don't agree with the people in the church down the street, or maybe with the person you share a pew with. You are worried about how you're going to pay the rent, pay for childcare, pay your medical bills, and pay for college. You are worried about how you're going to appear to the people you respect. Your church's worship seems stale. Or it seems vibrant, but it's the only part of your week that does. You are worried about terrorism and gun violence. You are worried about job security. I know you are worried about denominational decline. I know you are seeing statistics all the time about Millenials not attending church anymore. I know you've been given reason after reason why that is—some from developers of surveys, some from young people themselves. Or you are a Millenial, and you're sick to death of people talking about your [lack of] church attendance. There is a lot to worry about. I'm worried, too. But I also have hope. I always have hope.

No matter what we face in our lives, as members of the Body of Christ, we never face it alone. There is an oft-quoted saying that no one can be Christian alone. This is true. There is no such thing. You are never alone. When you sit in your pew on Sunday and confess in the silent prayer time that you struggle with an addiction to pornography, shopping, alcohol, drugs, or other people's compliments, even then you are not alone. Even if no one knows your difficulties, you do not face them alone. You are a member of the Body of Christ. Whatever you do and whatever you face, you do so with Christ, in whom you have your life. And you do so with your siblings who are members of Christ's body with you. This is what it means to be baptized into this wonderful, messy, complicated, and beautiful Church.

What this also means, is that the adolescents who are in our churches need us to step up and be their allies. They were the cute kids we laughed with (at?) during the Children's sermon years ago. They were the ones we proudly patted on the back after their flawless performance as sheep in the Christmas pageant. They were the ones we greeted with applause when, as an infant, they were carried through the aisles of our church on the day we promised to help them grow in the love of Christ and in their journey of discipleship. Just because they started to grow breasts, go through a growth spurt that made them awkward and clumsy, or haven't quite figured out deodorant yet, doesn't mean we get to ignore them until they become more palatable to us. The church is supposed to be messy because people are messy (admit it, you reading this are also). They are facing things we know nothing about; but we could. They are our siblings, and they need us. We need them, too.

I have been an adult now for a while. I have educational debt, and a mortgage. I have children. I have degrees and letters after my name. And here's what I've learned about being an adult: it's hard. There are days when I have to let my tears flow because of how life happens. I am disappointed and frustrated. I am angry at the difficulties I have had to endure in my life. I am angry at the difficulties others have had to endure. I grieve about poverty and feel powerless to do anything about it. I am angry at my denomination's continuing abuse of its LGBTQI+ members and allies. I hate addiction. I hate violence. I hate sexism, racism, heterosexism, ageism, and sizeism. Sometimes I hate having to be responsible. I thought being an adult would be easier. I need what our adolescents need. I need all of you.

We all need people who are going to welcome us for who we are, hear our stories, and help us face what it is in life that is so hard. If it is true, and I believe that it is in part because of what I read in Scripture, that we are not in this alone, then this is a foundational call of being Christian. So let's do this together. Really.

Share your story. Don't confess only in the silent prayer time, confess out loud to your small group or your Sunday school class. If those spaces are not safe for you to share your story with, seek a trusted member of the church to help you create that kind of space. We all need places we can share openly and honestly. When you have that space, confess that your life is hard, and you need help. When you hear someone's confession, know that because you share a Body with them, it is your struggle now, too. When a young person shows up at church, don't shame them for not being there more often or for wearing the "wrong" clothing or for not participating in worship like you do. Instead, ask them how they are and invite their stories. Truly welcome them, and listen without judgment. Youth, be courageous and share your stories and yourselves with your church. Don't roll your eyes at people who "just don't get it;" instead, help them "get it." Use your voice to call out the church for the ways you see it falling short. Adults, hear that critique and take it seriously. Partner with young people bringing their critiques. Help them use and amplify their voice. Preachers, and I speak as one, stop preaching every Sunday and sometimes help facilitate real conversations between the people in your pews instead. If we are only looking at the backs of the people who sit in front of us, how are we being the Body?

And since I mentioned clothing, the adolescent girls in our congregations do not appreciate the looks of disapproval or the whispers we think they can't hear about their "inappropriate" choices. Their bodies are beautiful and scared and created by God. They are not sexual objects and shouldn't be treated like they are. They don't come to worship to be criticized or shamed for having their beautiful bodies, they come for the same reason you do—for worship, for community, for truth, for inspiration, and for strength for their journeys. Trust them with their own bodies.

Here's another thing our young people need from church—they need to know that you are with them in their fight against the forces that threaten their living whole and healthy lives. I'm talking about Sin. I know most of us have been raised to think about sin as something a person does that is wrong in some way—something that is against God's will or something that isn't loving toward neighbor and self. This is true. *But sinning is not all there is to Sin.* Sin is also something outside of each of us, something that is holding onto control in this world even though Jesus came and destroyed it by dying on the cross and then being resurrected three days later. Sin is what tells young people that they are worthless. Sin is what tells adults to think young people are worthless. Sin is what weasels its way into our churches so that we start thinking of adolescent girls as sex objects, just like the marketing industry does. Sin does all this and more. Now, I love the church. I really love the church. And so does God. The church is a scared and blessed gathering of folks commissioned to help build the kin-dom of God and infused with the Holy Spirit and distributors of grace. But I can see that the church is not immune from Sin's power. I wish it were. I wish it was the place we could all go to get away from Sin's power. But the truth is that this side of the new creation, we are not immune from Sin's power no matter where we are. It is also true that we can partner with each other and work with God against Sin, participating in its final demise.

How do we do that? We do it by the grace of God. We do it through the power of the Holy Spirit. We do it as the Body of Christ who knows that Sin cannot and does not win because Death does not have the last word. Love and life do. Concretely, we do it by knowing and loving each other, starting with those in our own churches. I don't watch a ton of reality television, but I did watch the first season of *Survivor*. From what I understand, this was the beginning of the whole reality TV craze (well, if you don't count MTV's *The Real World*). During that season, some of the survivors formed an alliance with each other to work together and to vote others off the island strategically to increase their chances of staying in the game. We need an alliance between the adults and the youth in our churches, not to keep them from being voted off the island, but to keep us all in the Body of Christ and working on God's team against Sin. We need an alliance, not against other participants in God's creation, but against Sin. We can trust that Sin won't win because of Jesus Christ. We can partner with each other against Sin's trying to occupy our lives, and we can do this because we are together in the Body of Christ. Sin is strong but Christ is stronger, and it is in Christ that we live, move, and have our being (Acts 17:28).

When a girl in our church is struggling with her body image, the church should welcome her struggle without judgment, with compassion and grace, and with the commitment to help her see where Sin is trying to work against her wholeness and well-being. The church can help her interpret her struggle differently and can give her tools to combat the struggle, and enter into that struggle with her. When a girl is afraid that the immigration status of her parents might cause them to be deported, the church can help her see where Sin might find a foothold in her fear and can help give her courage and an immigration lawyer for her family. The church is capable of being in an alliance with its members, no matter their age, gender, sexual orientation or gender identity, immigration status, or race or anything else that divides people these days. Because we are all members of one Body together. Therefore it is our responsibility to care for each of those members personally and actively.

While this applies to everyone in the church, there is special importance for women and girls forming an alliance with each other. Adult women have been facing the force of sexism and the myriad ways it shows up in their experiences for their whole lives. They are in a unique position to respond to the struggle of girls. Moreover, sisterhood between women of different ages is a powerful and sacred opportunity for sharing in life together—the difficulties and the celebrations. Women and girls are on the same side, can learn from one another, and can strategize together. Moreover, sometimes women and girls will need to be united together to fight against how men and boys are treating them or view them. Women and girls can form a foundational alliance together, and can be a base that men and boys can also join as the whole church body becomes more closely united against the outside force of Sin. A closely united church body fighting against Sin is so powerful, because it is the power of God in action in the here and now.

No matter what worries we have, no matter how difficult life is, no matter how strong we think Sin might be, we can have a deep and unfaltering hope. This is the hope that I have for how we as the church can function in this world. When I am frustrated by the church, I have hope. When I see Sin at work in the people and places I love, I have hope. I have hope because of who Christ is in this world. I have hope because I have listened to the stories of adolescent girls from their lives and they are bright, interested, passionate, thoughtful, and resilient. I have hope because when I listen to them, it makes a space for grace to enter into their stories. When you, adolescent girls, listen to my stories, I too experience grace. I have hope because I know that Christ didn't stay dead. I have hope because the Spirit won't let me despair. I have hope because I have seen evidence of the kind of alliances we need, and they are more powerful than the hatred, fear, and ignorance against which we fight. Our alliance is not only with one another, but also with God. And God cannot fail. Nor can the Body of Christ die, because it has already been resurrected.

I close this letter with the confidence that you can act in this hope and in the power of God. I implore you to listen carefully and intentionally to one another. Welcome each other's pain and struggle into the space that is the Body of Christ in your local congregations. Connect yourselves in the fight against the ways Sin shows up in your lives and in your church. Remember, you are more powerful than Sin because Jesus defeated Sin on the cross. While we wait for the kin-dom to be fully realized, for all remaining evidence of the old age to be gone, we can participate with Christ in the defeat of Sin because this is who we are, we are the ones who live in Christ and live with one another for the purpose of setting the captives free and liberating those who are oppressed (Isa 61:1 and Luke 4:18).

Thank you for reading my words, may you now listen to the words of your siblings in Christ, particularly those who are adolescent girls. In the power of Christ, in whom I live as a baptized believer, and through the grace of God, I write with sincerity and hope.

APPENDIX

MY INTERVIEW PROTOCOL FOR this project was approved by Duke University's Institutional Review Board in May of 2013. I traveled from my house about an hour north of New York City all around the New York Annual Conference of the United Methodist Church, seeking to hear from adolescent girls about their lives and their faith. The interviews were conducted in spaces the girls requested. Some were in their churches, some were in public spaces like cafes or coffee shops, some were in the homes of their youth workers. Of the 24 girls I spoke with, 13 were interviewed in groups of 2-5. The others were interviewed one-on-one. Initially, I envisioned only doing one-on-one interviews enabling me to hear more stories from each girl's life. However, some of the girls requested to speak with me in groups. The first group interview I did was with two girls, who expressed clearly that they would be more comfortable interviewing together rather than separately. I did so as a kind of experiment, knowing I could simply choose to not use the interview if it turned out to not work as well as a one-on-one interview. As our conversation progressed, I learned that one of the girls suffered from selective mutism, a psychological condition that rendered her unable to speak during specific times of stress or anxiety or with specific people.[1] When she was unable to speak to someone, the other girl was her mouthpiece – the one person to whom she could vocalize her thoughts. This had been the case since childhood, and the two girls were now seniors in high school. Clearly, she was someone who benefited from the presence of her friend during a research process that involved

1. Vorvick and Merrill, "Selective Mutism," *National Institutes of Health*, http://www. nlm.nih.gov/medlineplus/ency/article/001546.htm.

speaking.[2] After this first test group interview, I offered the option for a group interview if a girl, her parent/caregiver, or youth minister asked if it was a possibility.

In efforts to respect the girls and the stories they shared, I tried to level the asymmetry of power between myself and the respondents in some key intentional ways.[3] This power came from my being a middle class, white adult, and authority figure in the church as an ordained clergywoman. I was very aware that these girls were taking time away from their lives, mainly from their summer vacations or summer employment, to help me with my research. I thanked them for their participation. I began and ended each interview with time for the girls to ask questions of me. Sometimes these questions were seeking more information about my project. Sometimes these questions were about why I wanted to interview them. Sometimes they had no questions. In two different interviews with groups of Black girls, I was asked if I had experienced racism, a question that did not come up in my interviews with white girls. Some of the girls asked if they would be able to read my book when it was complete.

The girls also thanked me for interviewing them. I designed my interview questions into three groups. The first was basic background information, the second was religious life, and the third was more in-depth

2. In their chapter, "Writing on Cellophane: Studying teen women's sexual desires, inventing methodological release points," in *The Methodological Dilemma*, Sara I. McClelland and Michelle Fine make the argument that speaking with girls in groups is sometimes a better methodology than one-on-one. They argue that, "Wrapped in a kind of *collective discursive cellophane*, we believe it may be difficult for [teen women] to speak as their tongues are weighed down with dominant assumptions and panics; and, similarly, our ears may be clogged with our own dominant (feminist) discourses for their desires" (232, italics original). McClelland and Fine are writing about their methodology of studying teen women's sexual desires. Among the many suggestions they offer for how to do such research, they note the collective wisdom of girls and the way girls will encourage the conversation forward, adding to each other's comments in a group setting. The authors' argument about girls' assumptions and my own expectations and desires for our conversations about their life and faith rang true.

3. Elliot G. Mishler, Professor of Social Psychology at Harvard University wrote an important book on interviewing from his perspective as a scholar of narrative psychology. He wrote, "In the mainstream tradition the interview-interviewer relations is marked by a striking asymmetry of power, this is the central structuring feature of interviews as research contexts," *Research Interviewing*, 117. Mishler argues that empowering respondents in the interview situation tends to produce narrative accounts as they speak, and that, importantly, "through their narratives people may be moved beyond the text to the possibilities of action" ibid., 119. These interviews were not an end in and of themselves; I sincerely hope that sharing their stories open up possibilities for action in their lives.

questions about their experiences. Although the questions served as a guide for the interviews, I was not bound by them. Because I am interested in liberative ministry with girls and Paul as a resource for this ministry, it was important to me that the interview process itself be a practice of freedom. Encouraging narrative and viewing the interview time as a time of conversation between myself and the girls was part of putting into practice the theology explored in this paper.

The anonymity of the girls is preserved; no real names or specific locations within the New York Annual Conference are used in this paper. This practice of maintaining anonymity of respondents is controversial.[4] I did not therefore take the decision to opt for anonymity lightly. In the interest of protecting the privacy of the girls, all of whom were extremely open and honest with me, I determined that using pseudonyms would be the best course of action. Rather than assigning them a name, because names carry so much cultural and personal connection, I asked each girl to choose her own name. Many of the girls were excited about this part of the process. They often had names that they wish were their names and were excited to use them. Some of them picked the names of their heroes from television or the music industry. Only a few seemed to struggle to find a pseudonym. The pseudonym of "Lena" for one of the interview participants was my own creation because I forgot to ask her at the time of interview. All others were the choices of the girls interviewed.

The most important part of this project is offering a space for adolescent girls to share their stories of life and faith. As I sat down with each girl I interviewed, I wanted to create a space where they were free to voice their opinions, questions, beliefs, unbeliefs, and experiences. I was eager to hear from them, and came into each conversation not knowing at all what I was going to get. Many of the girls I had never met before. Even the girls with whom I had been in ministry in the past, had grown since I last had significant conversations with them. I sought to begin conversations with openness from my end, ready to welcome whatever they chose to share.

When girls shared painful realities with me, I grieved that I was not their pastor and would not have opportunities to follow up with them. In one interview, I could not help but pray with and for the girl with whom I was talking. It seemed the only responsible way to treat her with sensitivity

---

4. Mischler points out that while sometimes confidentiality is "consistent with the aim of empowering respondents," sometimes it instead reinforces the decontextualization that is a part of an interview process and deprives them "of their own voices," ibid., 125.

and to value and respect the pain she had shared with me. Adolescence, no less than any other life stage, involves moments of joy and moments of sorrow, times when faith is sure and times when faith is shaky. My firm hope is that the way I present their stories and experiences honors the people they are. My trust is that the reader will listen with integrity and generosity. These are the stories of the girls in our churches, these are members of the Body of Christ with the rest of us.

INTERVIEW QUESTIONS

The following was my list of questions that guided my interviews. Sometimes our conversations followed quite closely the questions I have listed here. Sometimes these questions served as a launching pad for a conversation that went somewhere I could not have anticipated. These simple questions offer an easy way to begin to hear the stories of adolescent girls. I share them here in hopes that these may be a kind of guide for those who are looking at creating space for meaningful conversations with adolescent girls. These are questions to ask them; these are questions they can ask you.

- How old are you?
- Who do you live with?
- What is the place where you live like? Is it an apartment? A house?
- How do you describe your ethnicity?
- How do you describe your sexuality?
- Do you have a job after school or on weekends?
- Do your parents/caregivers work outside the home? If so, what do they do?
- How long have you been attending your current church?
- Why did you start attending your current church?
- Are you a member of that church? Have you gone through Confirmation?
- What do you like about your church?
- What do you wish was different about your church?
- How has your time in this church affected or not affected your faith? What about your time in other churches?

- What would you say are your faith commitments? What do you believe?
- Do you believe in God?
- What do you think God is like?
- Who is Jesus for you?
- Who is the Holy Spirit for you?
- What do you think Christianity is all about?
- Have you had a conversion experience? If so, what was that like?
- What or who helps you in your faith journey?
- What or who makes your faith journey more difficult?
- What do you think sin is?
- How did you come to think of sin in this way?
- How do you define evil?
- How do you define temptation?
- How would you describe your faith?
- What do you believe about God and Jesus?
- What are your hopes and dreams for your future?
- What do you think might help you reach your hopes and dreams?
- What might get in the way of you reaching your hopes and dreams?
- What are your biggest fears?
- What makes you angry?
- What makes you happy?
- What do you like to do for fun?
- What do you think you'll be doing in 5 years? In 10 years?
- What five words would you use to describe yourself?
- What do you think sexism is?
- What do you think racism is?
- What do you think it means to be a girl or woman in the church?
- What kinds of things have you seen a woman or girl do in church leadership?

- What kind of clothes do you wear to school? Are they different than clothes you wear to church? Are they different than the clothes you wear to a party? Why or why not?

- Follow-up: How do you feel when you wear different clothes – how do you feel when you wear school clothes? Party clothes? Church clothes?

- Are there clothes girls should or shouldn't wear to church? Why or why not?

- What does it mean to you to become a woman?

- What can a girl be when she grows up?

- What do you think makes a woman a "woman of God" or a "woman of faith?"

- What makes a girl a good Christian?

- How does one become a good Christian?

BIBLIOGRAPHY

American Psychological Association. *Developing Adolescents: A Reference for Professionals.* Washington, D.C.: American Psychological Association, 2002.

Arnett, Jeffrey Jenson. "Adolescent Storm and Stress, Reconsidered." *American Psychologist* 54 (May 1999) 317–26.

————. *Emerging Adulthood: The Winding Road from the Late Teens through the Twenties.* New York: Oxford University Press, 2004.

Astley, Jeff, and Colin Crowder. "Theological Perspectives on Christian Education: An Overview." In *Theological Perspectives on Christian Formation: A Reader on Theology and Christian Education,* edited by Jeff Astley, Leslie J. Francis, and Colin Crowder, x–xix. Grand Rapids: Eerdmans, 1996.

Baker, Dori Grinenko. *Doing Girlfriend Theology: God-Talk with Young Women.* Cleveland: Pilgrim, 2005.

Baker, Dori Grinenko, and Joyce Ann Mercer. *Lives to Offer: Accompanying Youth on Their Vocational Quests.* Youth Ministry Alternatives. Cleveland: Pilgrim, 2007.

Barclay, John M. G. "Introduction." In *Divine and Human Agency in Paul and His Cultural Environment,* edited by John M. G. Barclay and Simon Gathercole, 1–8. New York: T. & T. Clark, 2008.

Bareilles, Sara. "Eden." *The Blessed Unrest.* Epic, B00CF7PG5U, 2012, compact disc.

Beaudoin, Tom. *Consuming Faith: Integrating Who We Are with What We Buy.* New York: Sheed & Ward, 2003.

Bishop, Russell. "Soul-Talk: The Myth of the Spiritual Path." *Huffington Post,* April 9, 2012. http://www.huffingtonpost.com/russell-bishop/soul-talk_b_1410970.html.

Blodgett, Barbara J. *Constructing the Erotic: Sexual Ethics and Adolescent Girls.* Cleveland: Pilgrim, 2002.

Brown, Alexandra. *Cross and Human Transformation: Paul's Apocalyptic Word in 1 Corinthians.* Minneapolis: Fortress, 1995.

Brown, Lyn Mikel. *Raising Their Voices: The Politics of Girls' Anger.* Cambridge: Harvard University Press, 1998.

Brueggemann, Walter. *The Prophetic Imagination.* Philadelphia: Fortress, 1978.

Brumberg, Joan Jacobs. *The Body Project: An Intimate History of American Girls.* New York: Vintage, 1997.

Castelli, Elizabeth A. *Imitating Paul: A Discourse of Power*. Edited by Danna Nolan Fewell and David M. Gunn. Literary Currents in Biblical Interpretation. Louisville: Westminster John Knox, 1991.

Copeland, M. Shawn. *Enfleshing Freedom: Body, Race, and Being*. Edited by Anthony B. Pinn and Katie G. Cannon. Innovations: African American Religious Thought. Minneapolis: Fortress, 2010.

Crain, Margaret Ann, and Jack Seymour. "The Ethnographer as Minister: Ethnographic Research in Ministry." *Religious Education* 91 (Summer 1996) 299–315.

de las Fuentas, Cynthia, and Melba J. T. Vasquez. "Immigrant Adolescent Girls of Color: Facing American Challenges." In *Beyond Appearance: A New Look at Adolescent Girls*, edited by Norine G. Johnson, Michael C. Roberts, and Judith Worell, 131–50. Washington, DC: American Psychological Association, 1999.

Dean, Kenda Creasy. *Almost Christian: What the Faith of Our Teenagers is Telling the American Church*. New York: Oxford University, 2010.

———. "Holding On to Our Kisses: The Hormonal Theology of Adolescence." In *The Theological Turn in Youth Ministry* by Andrew Root and Kenda Creasy Dean. Downers Grove, IL: InterVarsity, 2011.

———. *Practicing Passion: Youth and the Quest for a Passionate Church*. Grand Rapids: Eerdmans, 2004.

Dean, Kenda Creasy, and Ron Foster, *The Godbearing Life: The Art of Soul Tending for Youth Ministry*. Nashville: Upper Room, 1998.

DeVries, Mark. *Sustainable Youth Ministry: Why most youth ministry doesn't last and what your church can do about it*. Downers Grove, IL: InterVarsity, 2008.

Dewey, Caitlin. "Almost as many people use Facebook as live in the entire country of China." *The Washington Post*. October 29, 2014 and accessed January 6, 2015. http://www.washingtonpost.com/news/the-intersect/wp/2014/10/29/almost-as-many-people-use-facebook-as-live-in-the-entire-country-of-china/.

Duffy, David F. "Self-Injury." *Psychiatry* 8, no. 7 (July 2009) 237–40.

Dylan, Bob. "Gotta Serve Somebody" on *Slow Train Coming*. Original recording remastered. Sony, B00026WU6O, 2004, compact disc. Originally released 1979.

Eastman, Susan Grove. "Double Participation and the Responsible Self in Romans 5–8." In *Apocalyptic Paul: Cosmos and Anthropos in Romans 5–8*, edited Beverly Roberts Gaventa. 93–110. Waco: Baylor University Press, 2013.

———. *Recovering Paul's Mother Tongue: Language and Theology in Galatians*. Grand Rapids: Eerdmans, 2007.

Erickson, Erik H. *Identity: Youth and Crisis*. New York: W. W. Norton, 1968; Norton, 1994.

Farley, Wendy. *Gathering Those Driven Away: A Theology of Incarnation*. Louisville: Westminster John Knox, 2011.

Fowler, James W. *Stages of Faith: The Psychology of Human Development and the Quest for Meaning*. San Francisco: Harper, 1981; HarperCollins, 1995.

Freire, Paulo. *Pedagogy of the Oppressed*. 30th Anniversary Edition. Translated by Myra Bergman Ramos and with an introduction by Donaldo Macedo. New York: Continuum, 2001.

Fulkerson, Mary McClintock. *Places of Redemption: Theology for a Worldly Church*. New York: Oxford University Press, 2007.

Gaventa, Beverly Roberts. *Our Mother St. Paul*. Louisville: Westminster John Knox, 2007.

Groome, Thomas. *Sharing Faith: A Comprehensive Approach to Religious Education and Pastoral Ministry, The Way of Shared Praxis*. Eugene: Wipf & Stock, 1991.
———. *Will There Be Faith? A New Vision for Educating and Growing Disciples*. New York: HarperOne, 2011.
Haffner, Debra W. *Beyond the Big Talk: A Parent's Guide to Raising Sexually Healthy Teens from Middle School to High School and Beyond*. Rev. and updated ed. New York: Newmarket, 2008.
Hersch, Patricia. *A Tribe Apart: A Journey into the Heart of American Adolescence*. New York: Random House, 1999; Ballatine, 1999.
Heyward, Carter. *Touching Our Strength: The Erotic as Power and the Love of God*. New York: Harper & Row, 1989.
An Intermediate Greek-English Lexicon: Founded Upon the Seventh Edition of Liddell and Scott's Greek-English Lexicon. Oxford: Clarendon, 2003.
Jewett, Robert, assisted by Roy D. Kotansky. *Romans: A Commentary*. Edited by Eldon Jay Epp. Hermeneia—A Critical and Historical Commentary on the Bible. Minneapolis: Fortress, 2007.
Johnson, Norine G., and Michael C. Roberts. "Passage on the Wild River of Adolescence: Arriving Safely." In *Beyond Appearance: A New Look at Adolescent Girls*, edited by Norine G. Johnson, Michael C. Roberts, and Judith Worell, 3–18. Washington, DC: American Psychological Association, 1999.
Käsemann, Ernst. *Commentary on Romans*. Translated and edited by Geoffrey W. Bromiley. Grand Rapids: Eerdmans, 1980.
———. *New Testament Questions of Today*. Translated by W. J. Montague. Chapter XII translated by Wilifred R. Bunge. Philadelphia: Fortress, 1969.
———. *Perspectives on Paul*. Translated by Margarget Kohl. Philadelphia: Fortress, 1971.
Kinnaman David, and Gabe Lyons. *unChristian: What a New Generation Really Thinks about Christianity and Why It Matters*. Barna Group. Grand Rapids: Baker, 2007.
Kroger, Jane. *Identity in Adolescence: The balance between self and others*. Third Edition. Adolescence and Society Series, edited by John C. Coleman. New York: Routledge, 2004.
Loder, James E. *The Logic of the Spirit: Human Development in Theological Perspective*. San Francisco: Jossey-Bass, 1998.
Marin Lisa M., and Diane R. Halpern, "Pedagogy for developing critical thinking in adolescents: Explicit instruction produces greatest gains." *Thinking Skills and Creativity* 6 (2011) 1–13.
Martyn, J. Louis. "Epilogue: An Essay in Pauline Meta-ethics." In *Divine and Human Agency in Paul and His Cultural Environment*, edited by John M. G. Barclay and Simon Gathercole, 173–83. New York: T. & T. Clark, 2008.
———. *Galatians: A New Translation with Introduction and Commentary*. The Anchor Bible, edited by William Foxwell Albright and David Noel Freedman. New Haven, CT: Yale University Press, 1997.
———. *Theological Issues in the Letters of Paul*. Nashville: Abingdon, 1997.
McClelland, Sara I., and Michelle Fine. "Writing on Cellophane: Studying teen women's sexual desires, invention methodological release points." In *The Methodological Dilemma: Creative, Critical and Collaborative Approaches to Qualitative Research*, edited by Katherine Gallagher, 232–60. London: Routledge, 2008.
Mercer, Joyce. *Girltalk/Godtalk: Why Faith Matters to Teenage Girls—and Their Parents*. San Francisco: Jossey-Bass, 2008.

Meyer, Paul W. "The Worm at the Core of the Apple: Exegetical Reflections on Romans 7." In *The Conversation Continues: Studies in Paul in Honor of J. Louis Martyn*, 62–84. Nashville: Abingdon, 1990.

Miller, Lulu. "Trapped in his body for 12 years a man breaks free," *National Public Radio*. January 9, 2015 and accessed January 16, 2015. http://www.npr.org/blogs/health/2015/01/09/376084137/trapped-in-his-body-for-12-years-a-man-breaks-free.

Mishler, Elliot G. *Research Interviewing: Context and Narrative*. Cambridge: Harvard University Press, 1986.

Morton, Nelle. *The Journey is Home*. Boston: Beacon, 1985.

Muuss, Rolf E. "The Philosophical and Historical Roots of Theories of Adolescence." In *Adolescent Behavior and Society: A Book of Readings*, 1st ed., edited by Rolf E. Muuss, 3–22. New York: Random House, 1975.

Northcutt, Kay Bessler with Clinton Trench. "Bodies." In *Way to Live: Christian Practices for Teens* edited by Dorothy C. Bass and Don C. Richter, 31–46. Nashville: Upper Room, 2002.

Ohye Bonnie Y. and Jessica Henderson Daniel. "The 'Other' Adolescent Girls: Who Are They?" In *Beyond Appearance: A New Look at Adolescent Girls*, edited by Norine G. Johnson, Michael C. Roberts, and Judith Worell, 115–29. Washington, DC: American Psychological Association, 1999.

Osmer, Richard Robert. *The Teaching Ministry of Congregations*. Louisville: Westminster John Knox, 2005.

Palladino, Grace. *Teenagers: An American History*. New York: Basic, 1996.

Parker, Evelyn. "Introduction." In *The Sacred Selves of Adolescent Girls: Hard Stories of Race, Class, and Gender*, ed. Evelyn Parker, 1–13. Cleveland: Pilgrim, 2006.

———. *Trouble Don't Last Always: Empancipatory Hope Among African American Adolescents*. Cleveland: Pilgrim, 2003.

———, ed. *The Sacred Selves of Adolescent Girls: Hard Stories of Race, Class, and Gender*. Cleveland: Pilgrim, 2006.

Pearson, Allison. *I Think I Love You*. New York: Knopf, 2011.

Peck, Dawn H. "101 Ways to Fail School." Lecture at the University of Virginia, Charlottesville, VA, November 1988.

Powell, Kara E., and Chap Clark, *Sticky Faith: Everyday Ideas to Build Lasting Faith in Your Kids*. Grand Rapids: Zondervan, 2011.

Root, Andrew. *Revisiting Relational Youth Ministry: From a Strategy of Influence to a Theology of Incarnation*. Downers Grove: InterVarsity, 2007.

Root, Andrew, and Kenda Creasy Dean. *The Theological Turn in Youth Ministry*. Downers Grove: InterVarsity, 2011.

Sandberg, Sheryl, and Anna Maria Chávez, "Sheryl Sandberg and Anna Maria Chávez on 'Bossy,' the Other B-word." *Wall Street Journal*. Updated March 8, 2014 and accessed January 15, 2015, http://www.wsj.com/articles/SB10001424052702304360704579419150649284412.

Smith, Christian, with Melinda Lundquist Denton. *Soul Searching: The Religious and Spiritual Lives of American Teenagers*. New York: Oxford University Press, 2005.

The United Methodist Book of Discipline. Nashville: United Methodist Publishing House, 2012.

The United Methodist Hymnal: Book of United Methodist Worship. Nashville: United Methodist Publishing House, 1989.

Turpin, Katherine. *Branded: Adolescents Converting from Consumer Faith.* Youth Ministry Alternatives. Cleveland: Pilgrim, 2006.

Vorvick Linda J., and David B. Merrill. "Selective Mutism." *National Institutes of Health.* Updated February 11, 2012 and accessed December 31, 2013. http://www.nlm.nih.gov/medlineplus/ency/article/001546.htm.

Warren, Michael. *Youth, Gospel, Liberation.* New York: Harper & Row, 1987.

White, David F. *Practicing Discernment with Youth: A Transformative Youth Ministry Approach.* Youth Ministry Alternatives. Cleveland: Pilgrim, 2005.

Wolf, Naomi. *The Beauty Myth: How Images of Beauty Are Used Against Women.* Reprint ed. New York: Harper Collins, 2002.